NEW LOOK TO NOW

NEW LOOK

TO NOW

FRENCH HAUTE COUTURE   1947–1987

Stephen de Pietri and Melissa Leventon

with contributions by
Katell le Bourhis
Marie Andrée Jouve
Caroline Rennolds Milbank

The Fine Arts Museums of San Francisco
in association with
The Portland Art Museum, Oregon Art Institute

RIZZOLI
NEW YORK

New Look to Now: French Haute Couture 1947–1987 has been published in conjunction with an exhibition co-organized by The Fine Arts Museums of San Francisco and The Portland Art Museum, Oregon Art Institute.

The Fine Arts Museums of San Francisco
M. H. de Young Memorial Museum
June 10–August 27, 1989

The Portland Art Museum, Oregon Art Institute
December 13, 1989–February 4, 1990

The Powerhouse
Sydney, Australia
May–August 1990

The exhibition is made possible in San Francisco through a generous grant by I. Magnin and Lancôme Paris, and in Portland funds have principally been provided by Mr. and Mrs. Eric Hoffman.

Publication of this catalogue has been made possible by gifts from Mr. and Mrs. Eric Hoffman, Mrs. Vincent Hughes, and Mr. and Mrs. Christian de Guigné.

Copyright © 1989 by The Fine Arts Museums of San Francisco
First published in the United States of America in 1989 by
RIZZOLI INTERNATIONAL PUBLICATIONS, INC.
300 Park Avenue South
New York, NY 10010

Produced by the Publications Department, The Fine Arts Museum of San Francisco. Designed by Ed Marquand Book Design, Seattle. Photocomposed by Continental Typographics, Los Angeles. Printed by Dai Nippon, Tokyo.

Cover: *Dinner Dress*, Christian Dior, winter 1956 (no. 25).
Photo: Kaz Tsuruta.
Back cover: *Short Evening Dress*, Christian Dior, spring 1958, designed by Yves Saint Laurent (no. 30). Photo: Kaz Tsuruta.

Printed in Japan

Library of Congress Cataloging-in-Publication Data
De Pietri, Stephen
    New Look to Now
    Includes bibliographies.
    1. Costume design–France–History–20th century.   2. Costume design–United States–History–20th century.   3. Costume designers–France–History–20th century.   I. Leventon, Melissa.   II. Fine Arts Museums of San Francisco.   III. Title.
TT504.6.F7D4   1989   746.9′2′0944   89-7752
ISBN 0-8478-1139-5 (Rizzoli)

CONTENTS

FOREWORD

Costume is the most personal of the decorative arts. In this century it has become expressive of the self-image of the wearer within the contemporary aesthetic interpreted by a designer. The Parisian haute couture has been the sartorial measure of that ever-changing aesthetic for over a century, creating in each era a rich diversity of dress around common or parallel themes. *New Look to Now* chronicles forty years of near-circular change, acknowledging and celebrating our diverse aesthetic images of women.

New Look to Now was conceived in 1984 when Mrs. Eric Hoffman of Portland, Oregon, gave the Eleanor Christenson de Guigné collection of costume to The Fine Arts Museums. This collection, more than six hundred pieces strong, was assembled by the late Mrs. de Guigné from the early 1950s to her death in 1983. It epitomizes the fashionable woman of elegance of those years, and its presence in the Museums is a monument to Mrs. Hoffman's belief in costume as an art form. The exhibition as originally conceived focused on the de Guigné collection's highlights, and though it has subsequently expanded to include important costumes from other donors, the de Guigné collection remains its heart.

Other donors and lenders have contributed outstanding pieces to the exhibition to complement the de Guigné collection: Mrs. Eloise Heidland, Mrs. Vincent M. Hughes, I. Magnin & Co., Mrs. Thomas Kempner, Mrs. Clarence E. Knapp, Jeanne Magnin, Mrs. Mary Ritter, Mrs. Leslie L. Roos, Mrs. John N. Rosekrans, Jr., Cynthia and Lillian B. Schuman, Adele Simpson, and Mr. E.J. Larson. We are particularly grateful to *maisons* Givenchy, Grès, Lacroix, and Saint Laurent for their gifts of the 1987/1988 costumes that finish the exhibition.

The artistic force behind the exhibition is Guest Curator Stephen de Pietri. He has brought broad experience and an unerring eye to his task, which shows in both the exhibition design and the splendid catalogue photographs. The Fine Arts Museums' costume specialist, Assistant Curator of Textiles Melissa Leventon, has been involved in all phases of the exhibition, working closely with Mr. de Pietri to organize the exhibition and catalogue.

Textiles were organized into an independent department at the Museums in 1983, under the leadership of Curator Emerita Anna G. Bennett. Many of the acquisitions crucial to this exhibition were made during her tenure. Without Mrs. Bennett's drive and vision and the encouragement of her successor, Textiles Curator-in-Charge Cathryn M. Cootner, neither exhibition nor catalogue would have come to pass.

Support for this exhibition in Portland has been principally provided by Mr. and Mrs. Eric Hoffman. We wish to thank them for their extraordinary patronage of both The

Mrs. Christian de Guigné III wearing an evening dress from the winter 1965 collection of Madame Grès (Photo: *San Francisco Examiner*, January 1, 1966).

6

Fine Arts Museums of San Francisco and the Oregon Art Institute. Support for this exhibition in San Francisco has been provided jointly by I. Magnin and Lancôme Paris. We are delighted that I. Magnin has chosen to resume the tradition of sponsorship of these museums established by former I. Magnin president Grover Magnin.

Harry S. Parker III
Director of Museums
The Fine Arts Museums of San Francisco

Dan L. Monroe
President
Oregon Art Institute

ACKNOWLEDGMENTS

A project of this size and scope involves many hands, and we wish to extend special thanks to those people and institutions whose generosity has helped to bring this exhibition and catalogue to fruition. Foremost among the group is Mrs. Eric Hoffman; without her gift of the Eleanor Christenson de Guigné collection of costumes and her strong, steady support, this exhibition would never have happened. Mrs. Hoffman also helped to round out the exhibition by lending a number of costumes from her own collection. Our galleries were further enriched by the loans of several marvelous costumes from Mrs. John N. Rosekrans, Jr., and Cynthia and Lillian B. Schuman.

      The exhibition was put together on two continents. In France we were helped immeasurably by the following couture houses and their designers, directors, and employees: at Yves Saint Laurent by Mr. Saint Laurent, Pierre Bergé, Gabrielle Buchaert, Connie Uzzo, Isabelle de Courrèges, and Myriam Rollin; at Givenchy by Mr. de Givenchy and Dominic Sirop; at Pierre Balmain by Erik Mortensen, Jean-Louis Monjo, and Hervé Braillard; at Christian Lacroix by Mr. Lacroix, Jean-Jacques Picard, and Hélène de Mortemart; Sophie Jordan of Grès; Marie Andrée Jouve of Balenciaga; and Marine le Bourhis of Lanvin. Florence Müller of the Union Française des Arts du Costume and Guillaume Garnier of the Musée de la Mode et du Costume, Palais Galliera, have also given us assistance.

      In America, we are particularly grateful to Arlene C. Cooper; Harold Koda of the Fashion Institute of Technology, New York; Edward Maeder and Sandra Rosenbaum of the Los Angeles County Museum of Art; Robert Kauffmann of The Costume Institute, The Metropolitan Museum of Art.

      The catalogue has truly been a team effort. We thank Ed Marquand and Suzanne Kotz for its design and production, Kaz Tsuruta for his wonderful photographs, Diane M. Brush for the illustrations, and our co-authors—Marie

Andrée Jouve, Katell le Bourhis, and Caroline Rennolds Milbank—for making time for this project in their crowded schedules. For photograph-related matters we are grateful to Susan Train and Diana Edkins of The Condé Nast Publications Inc.; Carol Block and G. Lynn Fox of the Fashion Institute of Design and Merchandising, San Francisco; Betty Klarnet and Melissa Bedolis of *Harper's Bazaar*; Susanna van Langenberg of The National Magazine Company, London; Adelia Lines and her staff at the San Francisco Public Library; and Debra Cohen of Time, Inc.

Thanks must also go to Françoise Auguet, Gloria Duffy, Albert Elia, Margaret Geiss-Mooney, Craig W. Johnson, Lindsay Kefauver, Mrs. Marian Miller, Celeste Moreno, Mrs. Anne Sisson, Lewis Sykes, Margaret Van Buskirk, and Judith Zimrin.

Our deepest appreciation goes to the staff, trustees, docents, and volunteers of The Fine Arts Museums, who have done everything in their power to make this exhibition a success: Ian McKibbin White, Director Emeritus, under whom this project was conceived, and Harry S. Parker III, Director, who brought it to completion; Steven A. Nash, Associate Director and Chief Curator; Mrs. W. Robert Phillips, President of the Board of Trustees; the late Mrs. G. Gordon Bellis for her invaluable assistance in securing sponsorship; Ann Heath Karlstrom, Publications Manager, and Karen Kevorkian, Editor; Jean Neder, former Acting Curator in charge of the Textile Department; Leslie Melville Smith, Textiles Conservator, and Sarah Gates, Associate Textiles Conservator; Elisabeth Cornu, Objects Conservator; Joseph McDonald, Photographer; Debra Pughe, Exhibitions Support Manager; Bill White, Chief Museum Technician and Exhibition Designer, and his staff; Connie King, Christine McCullough, and Ron Rick, Design; Kittu Gates, Senior Registrar, and Thérèse Chen, Ted Greenberg, and Christopher Park of her staff; Julia Geist of the Textile Arts Council; and the unflagging interns and volunteers of the Textile departments: Mackenzie Anderson, Vicki Cabot, Nancy Cook, Susan Dangberg, Minerva de Jung, Natalie Edwards, Mary Huntington, Edda Ilyin, Nancy Love, Priscilla Miller, Kathy Murphy, Barbara Nitzberg, Shelley Rideout, Jean Scardina, and Carol Voulkos.

S. de P.
M. J. L.

NEW LOOK TO NOW

Stephen de Pietri

SOME OBSERVATIONS ON COSTUME IN MUSEUMS

One of the most intriguing developments in the museum world in the past two decades has been the emergence and proliferation of historical costume retrospectives. The demand for qualified curators and specialized lighting and exhibition designers for these projects can hardly be met. Every major museum, if it had not originally a costume collection, has developed one. Interestingly, many of these institutions focus on pieces from the twentieth century. Of all the reasons that could account for this emphasis, it is perhaps significant that, in a century that has noted a diminishing number of artisans, haute couture represents the last concerted efforts of skilled craftsmen working in traditional forms, with vitality, on a large scale. Thus, costume as a decorative art has come into its own. Its popularity as an event, spearheaded by Diana Vreeland at The Metropolitan Museum of Art's Costume Institute in the early seventies, has shown no sign of subsiding. Today, as pieces from the eighteenth and nineteenth centuries become harder and more expensive to acquire, sights have shifted to late twentieth-century retrospectives, and the post–World War II period especially remains a fresh and fertile market.

Is the public appeal of such exhibitions an intense interest in the most recent past or simply an exercise in nostalgia? Has the quality and substance of life begun to change so rapidly that an ensemble as recent as 1965 speaks of a society already past and different? We may be talking about a level of observation somewhere below art appreciation and somewhat above shopping. The context in a costume exhibition is always comprehensible—the human form. No other frame of reference is needed, as for fully appreciating sculpture or painting. Have we created a vast, easy-viewing entertainment?

There have been heated arguments as to the place of costume in the fine arts. But what can't be reconciled with the fine arts can be grouped with applied arts. If a silver spoon, a goblet, or a Turkish carpet are admissible art forms, why is a ballgown somehow suspect? Its status as a fashionable object should not disqualify it from being taken seriously, even if its form changes far more rapidly than that of an armchair. Experts do not fail to comment on the differences between a Boulle cabinet and one by Jacob Frères. The human spirit thrives on change. The aesthetic of the new constantly supersedes the established, and each object has its "moment in style." On a larger scale these developments in fashion reflect major social changes in thought and perception. It is often possible to trace the spirit of an age in all its plastic arts.

Fashions changed slowly for centuries, the cycle gradually accelerating as communications improved. By the eighteenth century, silhouette changes were visible at ten- to fifteen-year intervals. With the industrial revolution, the increasing availability of information to an ever-enlarging public eager to display its expanding wealth and power resulted in a constant stream of new, fashionable apparel. At present, the changes are so rapid that the latest news is superseded in less than a couple of months—the short skirt yields at once to trousers. With so much publicity implying change, there is in effect no change at all, and as a woman never has time to adjust her eye to the new trend she continues to wear what is comfortable. What can one say about a fashion period in which a woman can wear a skirt length anywhere between mid-thigh and ankle, any heel height, and a coat whatever length it comes from the rack? Somebody evidently is not doing his or her job. The all-powerful, all-seeing fashion editor of legend is gone. She, or he, is now at the mercy of major advertisers and mass-market surveys. Only, great fashion, like any great art, has never been created by the masses.

NEW LOOK TO NOW: WHY AND HOW?

When I first came to The Fine Arts Museums of San Francisco, it was to look at some pieces from the newly acquired Eleanor Christenson de Guigné bequest. At the time I was working on an Yves Saint Laurent retrospective and thought there might be some early Yves Saint Laurents for Dior in the collection. (At the death of Christian Dior in 1957, Saint Laurent was appointed his successor and designed there until 1961.) Such pieces are especially interesting, showing the young designer influenced by and thoroughly grounded in the principles and techniques of the House of Dior, yet also wanting to break out and experiment on his own.

I discovered that not only were there very good Saint Laurents in the Museums' collection, but also interesting and important Balenciagas, Grès, Diors, and many more. What intrigued me most were the examples from several couturiers for the same season, offering fascinating case studies in the ways different designers were expressing themselves at the same moment. The suggestion of organizing an exhibition with this collection was proposed.

With some further foraging through storage, I came up with a number of significant post–World War II Diors and Balmain and a rare bustle-back Balenciaga from 1947. The exhibition began to define itself. With the Eleanor Christenson de Guigné collection as a base, we would draw on other existing Fine Arts Museums objects, including donations from many prominent San Francisco women of style. At the same time we needed to pursue new additions, to flesh out our survey for the years from 1983 to 1987. For more than a year I worked in concert with Melissa Leventon, Assistant Curator of Textiles, searching for needed costumes and accessories, defining and fine-tuning the selections, and preparing material for the catalogue.

A bonus for the viewer in the last exhibition gallery are the four models from 1987. They have been donated to the Museums' permanent collection by the houses of Yves Saint Laurent, Hubert de Givenchy, Madame Grès, and Christian Lacroix. They represent the great traditions of the past, the present, and the continuing change and movement of the French haute couture.

THE SELECTION PROCESS

The actual process of selection for a costume exhibition is interesting perhaps because it is the least evident work in putting together a major retrospective. With over three hundred pieces to choose from and a final goal of one hundred in the finished exhibition, the editing phase begins at once. Obviously some pieces are so important, either by their notoriety or their influence on the fashions of the time, that they must be included without question. For most of the other ensembles, the task is less simple. Some sinister underground room is generally found (I have given up trying to fathom why all costume collections are subterranean), a sad and solitary mannequin is dragged in, and the rolling racks make their appearance. One by one the garments are tried on. Sometimes great discoveries are made: "It looked like a rag on the hanger, but it's heaven on the body"; sometimes great disasters, strange and wayward alterations and hemline changes: "The cocktail dress is from 1958 but was turned into a mini in 1965!" Each piece is studied, discussed, and dissected. Is it typical? Is it atypical? What does it say? Can we make it work with a great hat and lots of jewels? (Luckily the Museums have a windfall in the hat collection of Kay Larsen, which, copied from French models, literally mirrors the dates of our present exhibition.)

As with any editing job, there exists an idea beforehand of what points need to be made, but at the same time the concept must remain open for new influences and surprises.

For example, we had a number of short evening dresses from the Dior spring collection of 1958—the first collection designed by Yves Saint Laurent. It was known as the Trapeze because the dresses were cut to swing freely from the shoulders in an A-line without a waist indication. One particularly lovely dress from this collection was Baghdad, in beige tulle glitteringly embroidered in Eastern motifs. With a cinched waist and full skirt, the dress was obviously based on earlier Dior models and was decidedly looking back. It made a confusing statement with the newer trapeze looks and blurred the grouping. We decided to omit it. The choice is not always easy. It is not only the single dress that is important but often how the combined pieces in the exhibition interrelate. Will they evoke the period? Are the colors and forms too varied to be aesthetically cohesive? Is there a balance of both day and evening wear?

Along with these concerns, we are also attempting to date and research each piece. From newspapers to magazines, designer files and donor information, all sources are exploited. Sometimes the date of a piece is enough to include it in the final selection. For example, a lovely spangled tulle strapless ballgown by Balmain had been edited because it seemed an example of a rather typical evening dress of the early fifties. When it was discovered that the dress was actually purchased in 1947, it had to be reinstated, as neither its form nor fabric were typical for that early year. Dating, in a general way, is not too difficult, but there are always those annoying exceptions. Occasionally a style will surface, seemingly unrelated to what was happening in fashion. It may be the advance guard of a future collection, but sometimes a designer will hark back to something done years before. Couturiers like Gabrielle Chanel and Madame Grès defy precise dating; the styles they developed became classics and their art became the constant repetition and reinterpretation of a fashion formula. To organize our forty years of French haute couture we subdivided our time span into stylistic categories. Unfortunately, it never occurs that fashion changes neatly on the beginnings or endings of decades. The six chapters representing our divisions are, at best, our attempt to re-define the major trends from 1947 to 1987 and therefore more fully describe and understand the evolution of late twentieth-century style.

Stephen de Pietri is Guest Curator and Exhibition Designer, New Look to Now.

THE ELEGANT FIFTIES: WHEN FASHION WAS STILL A DICTATE

Katell le Bourhis

Since the eighteenth century, the arrogant world of French fashion has strongly influenced the way people have dressed the world over; since the time of Charles Frederick Worth in the nineteenth century, Paris has cast a long shadow over American style in dressing. Yet during World War II, when the City of Light was occupied by the Germans, the English and Americans were deprived of direct information from France. American dressmakers, fashion journalists, and ladies of style, trained to accept the dictates of Paris, were left to their own devices. This entirely new situation, as well as the restrictions and strife of a world at war, permitted American designers such as Claire McCardell to develop their own talent for casual wear and to succeed in establishing a strong, truly original American style.

During the war years, chic American women prided themselves in showing their sense of social consciousness and patriotism by dressing in an appropriately restrained manner. From their pre-war wardrobes, they relinquished the fantasy of their Schiaparellis or the grandeur of their Balenciagas. The mainstays of their wardrobes were almost identically tailored suits made of sensible, sturdy fabrics like tweed and worsted wool. The jacket was cleanly cut and worn over a plain skirt that just covered the knee. With broad shoulders as their only fashion characteristic, these are remembered as "Victory suits." Women used as little fabric and as few buttons as possible; this austerity became part of patriotic American chic. By the end of the war, the American woman's wardrobe had a masculine flavor.

Paris, February 12, 1947: In a definitely free but still very wounded city, Christian Dior, who had been working at Piguet and Lelong, showed his first collection to members of the fashion world who had hesitatingly returned, wondering what had happened to French creativity during the war years.

Mrs. Grover Magnin, exquisitely dressed by Dior, at a benefit for St. Joseph's Hospital, San Francisco, 1950.

The crowd, seated on gilded chairs in the pearl gray Louis XVI–style salon, rose with bursts of applause when the last model slipped backstage. Joining the suddenly enthusiastic crowd, Carmel Snow, the highly influential editor-in-chief of *Harper's Bazaar*, is reported to have said, "It's quite a revolution, dear Christian, your dresses have such a new look." Thus Carmel Snow's words started the legend. This was the "New Look" of dressing that the world would talk about and adopt with fervor. Once again, Paris became the center of fashion for stylish American women and the American fashion industry.

The new silhouette created by Dior was opposed to the conscious restraint of American fashion during the war years. Christian Dior presented extravagant femininity: enormous skirts using twenty to twenty-five yards of fabric flowed from pinched waists, reaching the ankle; softly dropping shoulders emphasized the generous roundness of the breast. It was an idealized nostalgia of curves and softness, a lavish fashion of quantity and opulence, a fashion made to please. Dior's first collection definitely alluded to things past, drawing upon the idealized femininity and security of La Belle Epoque.

Dior's New Look became an immediate triumph and was copied all over the world by everyone from expensive dressmakers to women sewing at home. In reaction to the shock and destruction of the war, the New Look corresponded perfectly to America's desire for security, represented by wealth and the traditional feminine and family values. In the early 1950s this taste for material comfort was enhanced by a great economic boom in America that, for the first time, profited people of many social levels.

Thus in the fifties America was on a shopping spree. Whether dressed in mass-produced garments or the couture clothes of the privileged, American women were locked into a hyper-feminine role. The success of their life was, as never before, tightly linked to advertisement, television, and magazines. Fashion became big news; *The New York Times* and the *Herald Tribune* sent fashion correspondents to Paris. *Harper's Bazaar*, headed by Carmel Snow, and *Vogue*, headed by Jessica Daves, prevailed as the fashion bibles of American women. Although the clothes of stylish American women of the fifties can be appreciated in museum exhibitions, it is instructive to go back to these contemporary sources of influence. A study of American *Vogue* of the fifties, for example, paying great attention not only to the fashion photographs but also to the advertisements and the lengthy editorial text, reveals why these clothes were fashionable, how they were worn, and what needs they fulfilled.

In 1954 the fashion editor Edna Chase, in her book *Always in Vogue*, recommended that the best way to become familiar with smart fashion was to have a "speaking acquaintance" with it. The young, aspiring, chic woman, privileged enough to have a social position, was advised to take advantage of every opportunity to observe the current mode correctly worn: she should go to the first nights of the theater and opera, and study snapshots of the newest styles in magazines.

Considering American *Vogue* as one of the strongest sources of fashion and social influence on American women in the fifties, a reader today might be surprised by the dictatorial tone of every article: from one season to another "One must . . . ," "One should . . . ," "Everyone does . . ." or "does not anymore. . . ." The woman of the fifties tended to be obedient and willing to accept the rules of the latest Paris fashions as interpreted by American journalists. Those accepted dictates produced an elegant, cohesive fashion and an overall non-individualistic picture, even though clothes and accessories were very often made to order. This is particularly striking in the social reviews of *Vogue*, which occupied a great deal of the magazine. In columns such as "What They Wore At" or "Carnet," every party from coast to coast is reported, and almost every woman photographed is wearing a strapless, full-skirted ballgown of pale colors, lavish fabrics, masses of tulle, beading, lace, and drapes. The scenes in these photographs have a certain elegant unity. For example, in November 1949 *Vogue* reviewed the San Francisco opera season and wrote,

> They [San Francisco society] support it, pamper it, and make a season of it. They take over the ten subscription evenings, give dinners, and dress mostly in Paris couture. San Francisco has a strong taste for French clothes and French food.

In May 1950, at a party given for the benefit of the St. Joseph Hospital, Mrs. Grover Magnin is pictured in "one of Dior's masterpieces." It was the sophisticated society woman whom *Vogue* used as a role model for women all over America. On the East Coast were Mrs. William Paley and Mrs. Winston Guest, and on the West Coast were Mrs. Christian de Guigné III, Mrs. Peter Thieriot, Mrs. Robert Watt Miller, and Mrs. Grover Magnin. These women were known only by their husband's names and were photographed for *Vogue* superbly dressed either at parties or in their own elegant homes or gardens, reminding us of charmingly poised and well-set late nineteenth-century portraiture. Today the fashion role models in *Vogue* include women achievers of every kind—entertainment, business, sport, and so on. But in the fifties a woman's achievement was evaluated by the man she married and her social grace. Thus, the clothes in the magazine reflected a conservative yet opulent elegance with little emphasis on youth or eccentricity, and the fashion text was rarely witty or tongue-in-cheek. It was a serious business!

Debutante Marian Miller dressed by Mad Carpentier for the Opera Ball, San Francisco, 1949.

One of the few original experiments in fashion during the 1950s was the creation of man-made fabrics, which were at the time highly praised and even found in Paris couture clothes. *Vogue* in April 1952 reported the use of synthetics by Dior, Fath, Balmain, Lanvin, and Heim.

With its authoritative tone, *Vogue* of the fifties shows us that the wardrobe of the chic American woman of that era was quite different from the wardrobe of the woman of the eighties. We now have mainly two kinds of day wear, casual and city/business, and two kinds of evening wear, for small evenings like cocktails and dinners, and for big evenings like benefits and balls. In the fifties clothes were strictly categorized for every occasion and time of day. Pre-war ideas on appropriate style were revived. Each season *Vogue* published textbook-like graphs, showing the new fashion according to the occasion. For evening wear, as noted in the November 1956 *Vogue*, four categories were named for which ladies of style would need appropriate clothes. Beginning at 5 p.m. was "Cocktails" dressing, followed by "Big Dinner at a Private House" dressing, then by clothes suitable for "Openings or Gala Theater," and finally by gowns for "Benefit Balls and Big Dances." The main differences during this decade among the various types of evening wear were the length of the skirt, the fabric used, the appropriateness of a hat, and the jewelry.

"Cocktails," which characterized every entertainment after 5 o'clock, called for short evening suits or dresses with matching coats, hats, clip earrings, "oceans of pearls," and brooches worn to the side. Clip earrings were an important accessory of the fifties. Geneviève Antoine Dariaux wrote in *Elegance*, "Pierced ears are unthinkable for an elegant woman and even more dreadful for a young girl." On April 15, 1959, *Vogue* noted that pierced earrings were outdated and went so far as to call them "a fetish." Surprisingly to us, in our more informal era of dress, in the fifties brocade, velvet, satin, taffeta, and faille were eminently appropriate as "after-five fabrics" since silk was not to be worn during the day. Also *Vogue* advised one needed to be eighteen years old to wear black, except for black velvet. If a chic woman wore a cocktail hat she also needed the appropriate cocktail gloves, an accessory to which *Vogue* devoted an entire article each season. The "obvious rule of thumb—the shorter the sleeve, the longer the glove" was advocated for cocktails, the medium four-button length in suede or glacé kidskin being recommended. For each cocktail dress an elegant lady would have a special small, fabric-covered handbag and high-heeled pumps, very often in suede or fabric dyed to match.

The "Big Dinner at a Private House" and the "Opening Gala and Theater" called for ankle-length but not too heavily crinolined skirts. Décolleté could be quite low, and strapless dresses were allowed if worn with a matching bolero or small fur cape, often in ermine or pale mink for the dinner. For the theater, as for the big balls, *Vogue* recommended mostly "Capes, capes, capes, all shapes and color!" throughout the fifties: long fur ones (sometimes in chinchilla), full-length cashmere or alpaca wool with satin lining, and three-quarter length in luxurious silk. *Vogue* also told the reader that evening gloves should not be removed when shaking hands at the theater and one should never wear jewels outside of gloves. *Vogue* also advocated the wearing of small hats to the theater, such as the well-remembered pillbox. In the fifties the rule was that whenever you wore gloves, you wore a hat, provided you were not at a ball.

For the "Benefit Ball" and "Big Dance," straplessness was de rigueur for married women. The well-bred debutante always wore a dress with straps or cap sleeves. By the mid-fifties dresses were cut extremely low, showing much back bareness. Huge skirts were often slightly trained; intricate gathers, drapes, and overskirts often amplified the behind. Stoles of matching fabrics or ephemeral chiffon or tulle wrap enhanced the femininity of the bare neck. Gloves, mostly of white or pale colored suede, glacé kid, or doeskin finish were recommended to be as high as the décolleté was low. These were highly sought after. Marshall Fields department stores were the first to retail the expensive Hermès gloves, which were then copied elsewhere. By 1956 the sheath ball dress was also "in"—a tall, wrapped column of luminous, pale chiffon, or a shining figure of satin or brocade with a single back panel hanging like a train.

Many rules were also noted for evening jewelry, as costume jewelry was considered a fashion accessory and not a piece of jewelry. After 8 p.m., wearing your diamonds was "a must" just as pearls were "a must" from lunch to cocktails. Since a diamond ring was the only form of diamond jewelry that could be correctly worn before lunch, diamonds were kept for the evening and preferably for ladies older than thirty. Before that age, a young fashionable lady was advised to only wear her diamond engagement ring. Diamond chokers, diamond clip-earrings, and heavy diamond bracelets were praised and flaunted. There are many advertisements for diamonds in *Vogue* of the fifties. For example, the DeBeers Diamond Mines, Harry Winston, and Van Cleef & Arpels urged women to buy diamonds; these ads are particularly noticeable at Christmas. Platinum settings were also pushed in the magazine advertisements. At this time, it was still fashionable for American women to smoke cigarettes. Jewelers designed intricate and feminine lighters and cigarette cases to accompany the precious compacts and lipstick cases, all to be placed in compartmentalized embroidered or beaded evening reticules. In 1953 the coronation of Queen Elizabeth II had a strong influence on jewelry worn at grand evenings by privileged American ladies of style; one saw a revival of the tiara at that time.

According to *Vogue* a lady of fashion in the fifties had to attend a mind-boggling list of special occasions during the day: Sunday lunches al fresco, ladies club and restaurant luncheons, afternoon tea, shopping, city weekends as opposed to country weekends, daylight dining, garden parties, mornings in town, horse shows, tennis matches, polo races, and so on. Television became popular (in 1954, although extremely expensive, there were already approximately a thousand color television sets in the homes of New York City elite), the game of Canasta became the rage, and appropriate dress for these new social occasions was also described in *Vogue*. Interestingly enough, the development of air-conditioning would call for more seasonless clothing. But the fifties thus were a time when the knowledge of intricate etiquette was still very much favored and discussed in magazines.

Revitalized with Christian Dior's New Look, elegant day wear in the early fifties consisted mainly of suits with femininely fitted jackets with pinched waists, and wide, long skirts; or quite prim, very covered-up dresses, again with the wide, long skirt, and, of course, the famous shirtwaist dress. The style set for day wear by Dior in 1947 evolved into Balenciaga's highly influential "Semi-fitted Look" in 1951; the cut of his coats and suits underlined the bust and waist in the front, while the back hung straight or slightly outward from the shoulders. With the reopening of Chanel in 1954, some of the far less structured, more fluid lines favored by Coco infiltrated the fashion scene. Yet, certainly for the most part, the fashion dictate for day wear, from suit to dress to coat, remained quite fitted with a marked waist and hip-length jacket. As the skirt narrowed quickly after the beginning of the fifties, particularly in the winter collections, a slit or short pleat on the back or the side allowed ease of motion to this constricting, tight fashion. Throughout this period summer dresses were gathered into the waistline with either a wide elastic or a narrow leather or fabric belt, and the skirt of the dress in its most extreme flared in full circle. In 1953, Dior revived the sheath dress, which remained popular as well for several years. And no matter the occasion—whether sporting, lunching, or shopping—elegant women from the late forties to nearly the end of the fifties would look poised and ladylike and never go out without a hat. *Vogue* reported, "She's hatted as surely as she is clothed, shod, gloved." In June 1956, the musical *My Fair Lady* was reported as a big influence and Ascot hats became the rage.

Besides being the year the turban experienced another comeback, the winter of 1957 is remembered in

Vogue as the winter of the leopard hat. Dior would even present a Somalian leopard fur blouse in his spring/summer collection. All through the fifties a great variety of furs were used to make coats, jackets, stoles, capes, hats, and trims not only for coats but also for suits and dresses. Persian lamb, Russian broadtail, beaver, jaguar, chinchilla, snow leopard, as well as natural mink were lavishly employed. Geneviève Antoine Dariaux wrote in *Elegance*, "Leopard is the most coveted fur in the world." Obviously, endangered animal species were not yet an issue. In 1950, over half of the advertisements for fur in *Vogue* were for sealskin. The coronation in May 1953 of Elizabeth II prompted a revival of white ermine, sometimes substituted for by white mink. Although mink was not the standard fur of the fifties, much was dyed experimentally to create such colors as silver blue, topaz, and black diamond.

Hairstyles in the early to mid-fifties were mainly variations of the French pleat (chignon) and the orderly, short, curled hairdo, both of which followed the natural smallness of the head. By the end of the fifties, exaggerated hairstyles such as the elaborate bouffant and beehive took the place of wearing hats. Yet even then *Vogue* recommended that hats remain a must for any service taking place in a church, such as weddings, funerals, and christenings, and for all diplomatic receptions as well as elegant cocktails and luncheons.

Short kid or suede gloves were always a part of the woman's day look in town, one-button length, slightly cuffed or slit at the wrist. For summer, the famous short white gloves are remembered as a trademark of the elegant fifties. Hand-stitched white piqué, linen, soft cotton, and nylon jersey knit were recommended for warm summer days, and white capeskin was kept for cooler summer days. The same summer dress worn without gloves would suddenly make it appropriate for a country weekend. Natural peccary skin or crocheted string and leather were preferred for fall weekends with tweedy outfits.

All through *Vogue* in the fifties, handbags were the subject of special articles as they too followed the rule of a different bag for each outfit and for each occasion. "Fashion demands a wardrobe of bags," stated *Vogue* to the elegant. A neat leather town bag always carried on the wrist was to be held at the hip as ornamentation. Large shoulder-strap bags were reserved for country weekends. Shoes, often made to order, followed the same rule and matched the bag for day wear or the dress fabric for evening wear. More functional than chic following the war, shoes by 1953 were subject to more fashion changes, with designers like Roger Vivier creating shoes with pointed toes and spike heels, in colors, of contrasting materials, and in innovative shapes.

Overall, the fashions of the fifties retained a heightened feminine shape for which foundations and lingerie were indispensable for molding the body. *Vogue* periodically reported on the new waist-cincher, waist-liner, girdle, or bra, referring to them strictly as foundation garments, while night-gowns, slips, and petticoats were called lingerie. If Paul Poiret is reputed to have liberated women from their corsets in the teens, Christian Dior is certainly responsible for putting women back into corsets, or at least into waist-cinchers, in 1947. Relief did not come until February 1958, when Yves Saint Laurent's first collection for Dior created the "trapeze" line, which hung down from the shoulder. *Vogue* reported in 1954 that girdles should be worn even under a bathing suit, if one wanted to achieve the proper line! In December 1954 Lily of France advertised lingerie especially made to fit under Dior clothes. That year over two hundred million girdles were sold in America, mostly of pastel color and synthetic rubber, which was developed during World War II and subsequently revolu-tionized the corsetry industry. *Vogue* also reported that the corset and brassiere stock in a good shop included about fifty sizes and several hundred styles by ten to twenty-five different makers. The pointed, under-wired merry widow bra was widely advertised in *Vogue*, in its natural or padded version. The slip followed the fashionable lengths and fullness of the skirts in real crinoline and skin-tight crepe de chine or nylon. When Yves Saint Laurent presented the trapeze line, a new cut of slip had to be created. After the war, nylon stockings replaced silk stockings; pantyhose remained non-existent throughout the fifties. In the late forties Hanes had begun to manufacture the new seamless stockings, but by the early fifties their popularity declined in favor of seamed stockings. In 1951 *Vogue* reported that most American women bought at least fourteen pairs of stockings a year; 648 million nylon stockings were produced in the year 1950 in America. Referred to as "nylons," the stockings were mostly in flesh tones or beiges, even if named "curried" or "taupe." The stockings were described by their denier and gauge, indicat-ing their sheerness. The lighter weight and tone prevailed in the evening. In a 1954 *Vogue*, Jacques Fath introduced the first patterned stocking in leopard print; Balenciaga tried to launch black sheer stockings, unsuccessfully, as they remained associated with mourning.

"The whole thing is a plot. The costume in all its parts. From suit to glove, scent to handbag, hat to shoe," said *Vogue* in March 1950. This was a time when American ladies of style willingly followed the dictates of the lively yet dog-matic fashion reports. In the fifties women composed their wardrobes according to the structure and etiquette devised by the fashion editors, who, for the last time in history, were almost exclusively influenced by Paris couture. It was also the decade when French couturier collections were nearly the

The ideal wardrobe of a woman of style for spring/summer 1957,
created by Christian Dior and presented by his house models.

sole source of inspiration for expensive ready-to-wear, mass-produced clothes, ladies sewing at home, and everything in-between. But since the end of the fifties the power to dictate fashion has extended beyond Paris to include London, New York, Milan, and Tokyo, and haute couture now shares its power with ready-to-wear designers. The style-consciousness of the eighties seems to place a premium on sleek, aggressive chic. The fashionable American ladies of the fifties seem contrived and obedient in their idealized hyper-feminine image. Yet the opulent refinement and poised style of that decade may call for us to hail it as the Elegant Fifties.

Katell le Bourhis is Associate Curator for Special Projects at The Costume Institute, The Metropolitan Museum of Art, New York.

Selected Bibliography

Bony, Anne. *Les Années 50*. Paris: Editions du Regard, 1982.

Chase, Edna, and Chase, Ilka. *Always in Vogue*. Garden City: Doubleday, 1954.

Dariaux, Genèvieve Antoine. *Elegance*. New York: Doubleday, 1964.

Hine, Thomas. *Populuxe*. New York: Alfred A. Knopf, 1986.

Hommage à Christian Dior 1947–1957. Paris: Union des Arts Décoratifs, 1986.

Vogue. New York: The Condé Nast Publications, Inc., 1939–1960.

SHOPPING FOR STYLE: COUTURE IN AMERICA

Melissa Leventon

In 1947 Europe was still recovering from the devastation of World War II. France had fallen to Germany early in the war and exported no fashions or information to America for four years. American designers, used to drawing information from European modes, were on their own and the designer ready-to-wear industry began to blossom. Yet, for many reasons, all eyes turned once again to France at war's end. In many ways the war had frozen fashion in time; it must have seemed perfectly natural to return to the pre-war status quo. Perhaps, too, the fashion ideas of the French couturiers were truly more attractive or exciting than were those of their American counterparts. Elements of the New Look appeared in the work of many designers before Dior first showed his version; historian Valerie Steele has suggested that Dior was the successful couturier because he brought a fresh, welcome excitement to fashion.[1] France worked hard to regain her footing by spreading fashion information as quickly and as excitingly as possible. Her grandest effort was the *Théâtre de la Mode*, a touring exhibition of 228 exquisitely dressed and bejewelled one-third-size fashion dolls. The dolls excited viewers in America—and elsewhere—to proclaim the miniature dresses prophetic of fashions to come.

American business played a major role in the post-war couture revival. Manufacturers and retailers must have suspected that the hiatus enforced by the war had not destroyed the status Paris fashions had enjoyed in America for over a century; it must quickly have been evident that Europe would once again dominate American fashion, as shrewd American manufacturers and retailers returned eagerly to France to buy couture and textiles. These Americans (and their customers) were among the few with money to spare for French luxury goods. And since the United States had dedicated herself to rebuilding Europe, American business could pride itself that its patronage brought needed funds to war-torn France. These Americans formed a large percentage of the couture clientele, and their growing friendships with some of the couturiers even more firmly cemented such patronage. American newspapers and magazines lauded several, among them San Franciscans Grover Magnin of I. Magnin & Co. and Adolph Schuman of Lilli Ann, as saviors of the entire French fashion industry. The French government shared this opinion, awarding both men the Legion of Honor for their services to French fashion and textiles. However, Dior noted that the war had changed American buying patterns. Americans no longer bought by the hundreds but rather by the tens, choosing only those models expected to be most commercially successful. Most would use their purchases for direct copies or to inspire home-grown designs.

Of course, it was not to be expected that all Americans would welcome the clothes that Paris designed. By and large, though, the protests were individual rather than corporate. Christian Dior, on his first visit to the United States in 1947, was surprised by what he felt was a hostile reception from some of the New York press and by an anti–New Look demonstration in Chicago. His crime—designing dresses that concealed American women's legs. In his autobiography, Dior also recalls some of the complaints he received by mail, including one from a garage owner in Los Angeles who threatened to tear Dior apart because the New Look had made his wife look like a Civil War–era stuffed doll.[2] Such resistance seems never to have been widespread, however, and Paris was very soon back on top.

Couture continued to inspire the look of the time until the mid-sixties, when dress embarked on a new course spurred by the rise of youth culture, the rebellious spirit that rejected the values espoused by the previous generation. Fashion began to draw its inspiration from the street instead of the salon, and couture fell on hard times: Balenciaga closed his doors and Yves Saint Laurent announced that he would abandon his twice-yearly couture collections in order to concentrate on his ready-to-wear line.[3] Ironically, it was Saint Laurent who, as the power of the street faded in the seventies, breathed new life into couture-with his ethnic collections.

Couture has continued to revive in the eighties, but it has never regained the position lost in the sixties. A shrinking clientele and rising prices mean that, more than ever before, it is supported by couturiers' ready-to-wear collections and licensing arrangements. Its role now seems that of a testing ground for new ideas or an effective advertisement for ready-to-wear and licensed lines. Americans are certainly still interested in couture. Newspapers and magazines still report on the collections and publish photographs of well-known women wearing couture dresses. According to *Harper's and Queen* editor Nicholas Coleridge, internationally prominent Americans—a handful of individuals rather than commercial clients—are still the mainstays of couture. However, as critic Holly Brubach has said, "The better part of what many, if not most, women know about fashion—about specific designers and current styles—they acquire by shopping."[4] A retailer is one of the conduits through which fashion designers reach their wearers. Without the patronage of stores such as I. Magnin, the New Look and subsequent couture-inspired fashions might never have become the overwhelming successes that they undoubtedly were.

Throughout this forty-year period, the percentage of American women purchasing haute couture has been quite small. A couture patron required money, leisure, a social life that provided opportunities for couture to be worn and appreciated, and the desire to be in the forefront of fashion. Extended trips to Europe, particularly during the summer, have been regular features of the year for many couture patrons, and a woman who met these requirements might travel to Paris once or twice a year to view the collections, spending several weeks there having her choices fitted. Once a couture house had a client's measurements, a mannequin could be built to replicate her figure, a tremendous time-saver. The wife of one American clothing manufacturer vividly recalled her first trip to Paris in September 1947. Her husband had preceded her by several weeks and selected dresses for her at several different houses. Mannequins were built using the measurements he had brought with him, and by the time she arrived her dresses were ready to be fitted.[5]

Until the mid-seventies, a woman who was not inclined, or not able, to go to Paris but who still wished to wear the latest French fashions, might avail herself of the custom salon at a handful of American department stores such as Bergdorf Goodman in New York and I. Magnin & Co. in San Francisco and Los Angeles. Couturiers permitted department stores and manufacturers to reproduce all or part of any model they purchased, and Magnin's custom salon offered faithful copies of a carefully chosen couture selection. Magnin's was the only department store in the western United States to offer this kind of service to its customers and attracted a clientele from all over the West Coast.

The process of buying a custom-made dress at I. Magnin & Co. was remarkably similar to that of purchasing a dress directly from a couture house. The season's collection would first be modeled for a client—nothing was ever displayed on a hanger—and she would make her choice. Details of fabrics, trim, and any alterations to be made in the design would be discussed with the director of the salon, Henriette Moon in San Francisco and Stella Hanania, universally known as Miss Stella, in Los Angeles. The same fabrics and trim used in the model were available, purchased by Magnin's from the couturiers' suppliers, but both Mrs. Moon and Miss Stella reputedly took care that no two women from the same social circle received identical dresses. The client would then be measured and a muslin pattern, a *toile*, was made. Clients'

Couture dresses were modeled while the customer relaxed in surroundings like these, in I. Magnin's San Francisco store, 1948.

This model from Yves Saint Laurent's Mondrian collection, winter 1965, was available at the custom salon at I. Magnin & Co. The label in its hem gives model and copy prices.

Dept. 280   Dia. S   St. Laurent - 83
                           Fall

violet & beige wool jersey mondrain dress

Original Price ————————————————— 1795.00

Copy Price ———————————————————— 795.00

measurements were kept on file, and for most, mannequins replicating their figures were built and kept. The client would return for fittings, usually three times but more if necessary. One Magnin employee remembers the dresses as being "almost made on the customer."

At its peak, the San Francisco salon employed a staff of nearly sixty fitters, seamstresses, and embroiderers. Both Mrs. Moon and Miss Stella were well known for their excellent taste and perfectionism, and the clothes the Magnin workrooms produced rivaled the French models in quality of finish; sometimes the "Magnin Custom" label was the only way to distinguish between them. Although clothes custom-made at Magnin's might have lacked the cachet of a couture label, they were considerably cheaper than their French-made counterparts. One Saint Laurent model purchased by the department store, which was donated to The Fine Arts Museums at the end of the winter 1965 season, still bears its custom-salon label listing prices for both the model and a copy. The French model cost more than twice as much as an American copy.

For women desiring to subscribe to the latest Paris mode but without the means to buy an original—or a wardrobe composed entirely of originals—the custom salon was a godsend. Fashionable San Franciscans would sometimes purchase a portion of a couture ensemble and have the rest made by the custom salon. Of course, one could simply buy the model from Magnin's rather than having it copied. Models remaining at the end of each season would be sold at a discount; any woman lucky enough to be model-size might be able to snap up a Paris-made bargain. Buying the original model from the couture house would preclude any copies being made. Buying a model through the department store, however, was no guarantee of exclusivity; other retailers or private clients could order the same model from the couturier. In theory, it was also possible, although unlikely, for the custom salon to continue to manufacture copies of a model after it had been sold, using the paper patterns supplied by the couturier.

As with one's Parisian *vendeuse*, the saleswoman who guides the couture client through every phase of the buying process, custom-salon clients often developed a friendship with the salon director. Many relied heavily on her taste in the choice of their clothes. Both Mrs. Moon and Miss Stella certainly purchased models at the Paris showings with Magnin's regular clientele in mind, and may also have purchased specific dresses for clients, making any necessary alterations in California once the outfit had been seen and approved.

Although the percentage of customers buying couture or patronizing the custom salon was small, couture was a powerful advertising tool for stores such as I. Magnin. American fashion magazines reporting on the collections ran photographs of couture models and mentioned the names of stores in which the models were available. Closer to home, at the beginning of each season Magnin's held a fashion show of newly arrived French models, which usually received heavy coverage in the local press. Even buying trips to Paris made news: a *Los Angeles Times* reporter nabbed Grover Magnin just off the plane from Paris to quiz him on the cut, colors, hemlines, and silhouettes of the winter 1949 Paris collections. Magnin's garnered a tremendous amount of press coverage that same season by buying two magnificent Dior ballgowns, "Venus" and "Junon," and announcing that they were museum pieces and not available for purchase. The dresses were instead modeled for three hours daily for the public to see and admire and at the end of the season were indeed donated to the M.H. de Young Memorial Museum.

The custom salon, which had opened before World War II, had reached its peak by the early fifties. Its fortunes were inevitably linked with those of couture: when the influence of couture lessened, the custom salon began a long, slow decline. By the time Mrs. Moon left I. Magnin in the mid-sixties, custom had decreased so much that Miss Stella was able to take on the management of the San Francisco salon in addition to her duties in Los Angeles, leaving Mrs. Moon's assistant to supervise day-to-day activities in San Francisco. Both salons had closed by the mid-seventies. The only "couture" I. Magnin and its counterparts carry today are the ready-to-wear lines designed by couturiers.

Melissa Leventon is Assistant Curator, Department of Textiles, The Fine Arts Museums of San Francisco.

Notes

1. Valerie Steele, *Paris Fashion, A Cultural History* (New York: Oxford University Press, 1988), 275.

2. Christian Dior, *Christian Dior and I*, trans. Antonia Fraser (New York: E. P. Dutton, 1957), 185.

3. See Ruth Lynam, ed., *Couture* (Garden City: Doubleday, 1972), 223–39.

4. Holly Brubach, "In Fashion," *The New Yorker*, 23 January 1989, 111–12.

5. Today, several couturiers send videotapes of their collections to far-flung clients, following up (in New York) with a small deputation from the *maison* to show some of the models and to fit dresses ordered. See Nicholas Coleridge, *The Fashion Conspiracy* (New York: Harper & Row, 1988), 178–79.

1947–1952 THE NEW LOOK: LAST GASP OF THE BELLE EPOQUE

The New Look was a term coined by Carmel Snow to describe the first collection of Christian Dior in spring 1947, but its influences were felt well into the early fifties. Its main attributes were the lengthening of skirts, narrowing of shoulders, cinching of waists, and padding of hips. New Look tendencies can be seen in the collections of 1945 and 1946, most prominently in the work of designers like Balenciaga, Jacques Fath, Pierre Balmain, and Lucien Lelong (for whom Dior worked and designed). But it was Dior in the end who is credited with giving free expression to this fashion revolution, a direct reaction to the Occupation, hard conditions, Utility wear, and shortages. It is no secret that the inspiration for the New Look was Dior's memories of his glamorous mother in the 1910s. One might argue that, after a half-century of war, a desperate attempt was being made to turn back the clock to an age of tranquility and elegance. Not only the Second World War but the first as well was pushed aside in a gasping reminiscence of the great days of the Belle Epoque.

That women chose to adopt these fashions, after very small resistance, to corset themselves and pad their busts and rumps as they had not done since the 1900s, says far more about the desire for change and need to express an aesthetic ideal than it does about the public's thoughts of progress or comfort. Chanel stated, with great vehemence, that it had taken her a lifetime to simplify and modernize women's clothes and that, within a couple of months, this man Dior had undone everything. For a number of reasons, nobody listened to Chanel at that moment.

Mrs. Grover Magnin dressed by
Christian Dior, ca. winter 1948 (no. 7)

Cristobal Balenciaga, winter 1947 (no. 2)

Left: Christian Dior,
winter 1948 (no. 8);
right: Christian Dior,
winter 1949 (no. 9)

Christian Dior, winter 1949 (nos. 10, 11)

Pierre Balmain, spring 1952 (no. 14)

1953–1957
THE FIFTIES:
BACKWARD
OR
FORWARD?

Somewhere sandwiched between the post-war boom and the death of Dior is fifties style. Sumptuous and cumbersome ballgowns directly out of the New Look continued, yet on the whole they were infused with an aerodynamic quality. Suits, hats, and collars at this time might well have been designed by van der Rohe or Saarinen. There was, by the mid-fifties, an almost mid-nineteenth-century bourgeois complacency. Money was there to be spent, and the war and its problems were pushed away by rampant consumerism. Women, as symbols of male power and money, were seen and not heard, wearing hats and gloves. The female figure, swelled out and uplifted, took on the aspect of the glistening space-age automobiles and appliances suddenly becoming available to everyone. A telling image can be culled from one of the many American science fiction films of the period. In *Invaders from Mars*, a blonde starlet in a strapless satin cocktail dress and high heels is pursued through the deserted streets of a destroyed modern city by a hulking extraterrestrial robot shooting death rays.

Bobby-soxers, teenage rebels, and rock and roll tentatively pointed toward a new, untapped market, and perhaps for the first time in the history of the world, the idea that youth might have something to offer was considered.

In 1954 Chanel reopened her salon, and though her initial efforts were not met with great enthusiasm, by the end of the decade her style, basically a reworking of her 1930s models, seemed uncluttered, modern, and new. By 1956, when Givenchy introduced the sack dress or chemise, things were looking very narrow indeed.

Cynthia Schuman wearing a youthful evening gown
by Pierre Balmain, spring 1953 collection (no. 16)

Christian Dior, winter 1956 (no. 25)

Pierre Balmain, winter 1955 (no. 20)

Yves Saint Laurent design for Christian Dior,
winter 1955 (no. 21)

Christian Dior,
winter 1956 (no. 24)

Cristobal Balenciaga,
winter 1954 (no. 17)

1958–1964 NEW WAVE

When the twenty-one-year-old Yves Saint Laurent took over at Christian Dior, the movement toward youth was already decided. Although the House of Dior eventually opted for a more conservative designer, the die had been cast, and it remained only for Saint Laurent to open his own house in 1962 to continue what he had started in 1958. By the late fifties the acquisitive innocence of the previous ten years seemed antiquated. Even if dresses were still boned and heavily constructed on the inside, on the exterior they glided smoothly over the body with an air of comfort and ease. Slim was the keynote—like a Giacometti. All of a sudden, doors were narrower, cars smaller, and suitcases flatter. For the first time a young, attractive couple was in the White House, and the First Lady, with a French background, obviously liked slim, simple clothes and was wont to sneak off to Chanel, Madame Grès, and Yves Saint Laurent. When she couldn't, she had them copied.

Stiletto heels, beehive hairdos, motorcycle jackets, black turtleneck sweaters, and leather and suede, up to that time the sole preserve of bohemians and beatniks, actually began to appear in the haute couture. This period, a fascinating transition, spans an era of tremendous change. From the cusp of the late fifties, it brings us to the edge of the youth movement of the mid-sixties.

Maggy Rouff, ca. 1958–59 (no. 32)

Left: Yves Saint Laurent design for Christian Dior,
spring 1958 (no. 28); *right:* Yves Saint Laurent
design for Christian Dior, spring 1958 (no. 30)

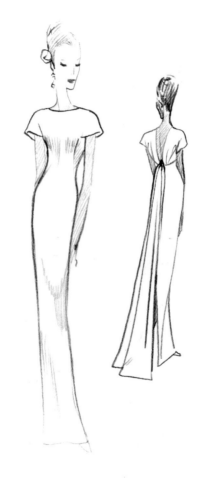

Cristobal Balenciaga, 1958 (no. 31)

Cristobal Balenciaga, spring 1965 (no. 47)

Mrs. John N. Rosekrans, Jr., in a sari-inspired gown by Cristobal Balenciaga, winter 1963 collection (no. 42)

Yves Saint Laurent design for Christian Dior,
winter 1959 (no. 34)

Yves Saint Laurent design for Christian Dior, spring 1960 (no. 35)

Cristobal Balenciaga, winter 1963 (no. 41)

Chanel, ca. 1960 and spring 1963 (nos. 37, 39)

Left:
Cristobal Balenciaga,
spring 1963 (no. 40);
right: Madame Grès,
winter 1964 (no. 43)

1965–1970 PLASTIC A-GO-GO TO HIPPIE COOL

That anyone in 1960 could possibly anticipate the changes that fashion would undergo in the next five years seems inconceivable. Even with the continuing influence of the youth culture that began in the fifties, it would have been hard to predict a fashion look based entirely on the young. Somebody saw the potential of a huge market and decided to exploit it—and it worked on both young and old. Within a matter of months, everything that wasn't new was out. New fabrics—vinyls, plastics, polyester doubleknits—new Day-Glo colors! The look was to the future with no compromise and no turning back. Young designers, the London mods on Carnaby Street, were leading the way. Names like Pierre Cardin, André Courrèges, and Paco Rabanne took the French into discotheques. Hemlines became the shortest in the history of fashion. The ideal image, with large hairdo, mini-dress, white stockings, and flat shoes, was that of a little girl. These child-women of all ages and their escorts in Nehru jackets and medallions go-goed and partied and drank and took drugs for a frenzied couple of years and then dropped. The pace was too much and, like the twenties, with which the sixties have so much in common, the moment destroyed itself by its very modernism.

By the time the mods were waning, another youth-oriented movement was ready to take its place, and though it is difficult to imagine a more opposed aesthetic, the trends somehow managed to co-exist for a brief time. By the late sixties, perhaps as a reaction to the super-fab, super-plastic mod, the hippie look made its appearance. Earth-based, braless and bare-legged, peace- and nature-loving, liberated and free, from Haight-Ashbury and Woodstock, the look was soon taken up by the fashion professionals. Cleaned up a little, it was presented on the runways in muted earth tones with maxi patchworks, flapping fringes, suede hot pants, and thigh-high boots—not a surprising development after the demonstrations in the United States and the French student riots of 1968, which profoundly changed Parisian society. The Rolls Royces were sent off to Deauville and everyone frizzed out their hair, grew beards if they could, and became "funky." Ethnic was the rage as alternative lifestyles and religions were explored by many. One-of-a-kind and handmade were what mattered. If they were worn-out and beat-up, so much the better (or chic-er).

Cristobal Balenciaga, winter 1966 (no. 56)

Cristobal Balenciaga, spring 1966 (no. 53)

Detail, Madame Grès, winter 1965 (no. 49)

Madame Grès, winter 1965 (no. 49)

Marc Bohan design for Christian Dior, winter 1966
(no. 57)

Cristobal Balenciaga, spring 1968 (no. 65)

Cristobal Balenciaga, winter 1967 (no. 61)

Cristobal Balenciaga, winter 1967 (no. 60)

Yves Saint Laurent, spring 1969 (no. 74)

Yves Saint Laurent, winter 1968 (no. 71)

Madame Grès, winter 1967 (no. 62)

Yves Saint Laurent, winter 1969 (no. 76)

1971–1975
RETRO:
EVERYTHING
OLD IS
NEW AGAIN

Somewhere during the late sixties between London and Paris, in the constant search for individual looks, new discoveries, and cheap chic, old bias-cut velvet gowns from the thirties, beaded flapper sheaths from the twenties, and platform shoes from the forties filtered their ways into the wardrobes of the young and trendy. Mixed with art-nouveau jewelry, head scarves, and Afghan coats, they expressed the funky hippie look to perfection. What began to happen by the early seventies was the gradual disposal of hippie accessories. What was left was the basic old dress. When Saint Laurent showed his forties collection in 1971 he was reviled by the press, yet it prophesied the next half-decade, and retro looks of the twenties, thirties, and at last the forties (all obviously with a seventies interpretation) were "the thing." When women forsook their bell-bottom pants and fun-fur chubbs for bias-cut crepe and rhinestones, fashion took a leap forward in terms of taste, but perhaps moved several steps backward for the Women's Movement. Does the liberated *femme fatale* exist?

Yves Saint Laurent, spring 1971 (no. 79)

Madame Grès, ca. 1971 (no. 81)

Madame Grès, ca. 1971 (no. 82)

Marc Bohan design for Christian Dior,
ca. 1972 (no. 83)

Madame Grès, ca. 1974, ca. 1980, ca. 1977,
ca. 1974 (nos. 85, 96, 92, 84)

1976–1987 THEATRICAL EXTRAVAGANCE

By 1976 the flagging fashion world was in desperate need of a boost. Tasteful, ladylike shirtwaists and tailored trouser suits were putting everyone to sleep. It was again Yves Saint Laurent who came to the rescue with his brilliant Ballets Russes collection. Like a second coming of Diaghilev, he set Paris ablaze using Russian and Eastern themes, rich brocades, fur, metallic chiffons, and gowns with huge skirts and full sleeves in a frenzy of opulent colors and textures. To these he added boots, turbans, and glittering jewels. He quickly followed with a Carmen-inspired collection and then one based on Imperial China. Obviously theatricality and extravagance were back in haute couture, and any designer who was not following was left behind. Fashion was fast becoming a public entertainment. The fear of ostentation, like a spectre of the sixties, was exorcized, and women began acting like divas from the 1950s, making grand entrances and large gestures. The same women who had parted their hair in the middle and worn jeans and peasant blouses were now in strapless gowns with long gloves.

In many ways the changes of the late seventies are still at work today. Haute couture has reestablished itself with great gusto. Designers have interpreted all sorts of exotic and historical themes, from the Renaissance to the eighteenth century, from Picasso to Surrealism. Accessories, almost in danger of extinction by the early seventies, have again become de rigueur for presentation—headpieces, hats, gloves, and sparkling parures now define and give expression to the designers' ultimate ideal.

It is not, however, through the haute couture collection, which barely breaks even with rising costs and diminishing clients, that the designer of today supports himself. If the collection is successful, it becomes the platform from which to sell the "image," which may include lower-priced ready-to-wear lines, accessories, and licensing from belts to sheets, towels, luggage, and cigarettes. Not to be forgotten, or in any way underestimated, are the hugely profitable cosmetic, beauty, and perfume lines. When Christian Lacroix opened his new couture house in 1987, the backers who put up more than ten million dollars were not hoping to recoup their investment by selling some expensive dresses. By 1988 two lower-priced collections and seven accessory lines had been developed, and that is, no doubt, only the beginning.

The future of the haute couture is uncertain. It is still a place where the richest or most extravagant women in the world can obtain clothes of a design and quality not obtainable elsewhere, made entirely to measure, with the added bonus that those who know will appreciate the cost. It is also a testing ground for new styles and techniques without the concerns of commercial reproduction. Its function as a publicity tool is evident, and its employment both directly and indirectly of hundreds and thousands of workers cannot be denied. It is doubtful whether, outside of the very few remaining houses where the traditions are scrupulously upheld, it can be compared to its glorious past. After the small handful of greats who still are at work decide to retire, one wonders if it can exist at all.

S. de P.

Yves Saint Laurent, spring 1977 (nos. 87, 88)

Yves Saint Laurent, spring 1983 (no. 101)

Yves Saint Laurent, spring 1982
(right: no. 98)

Left: Hubert de Givenchy,
winter 1987 (no. 102);
right: Yves Saint Laurent,
winter 1981 (no. 97)

Yves Saint Laurent, winter 1987 (no. 104)

Christian Lacroix, winter 1987 (no. 103)

CATALOGUE

Unless otherwise noted, all objects are from
The Eleanor Christenson de Guigné Collection
(Mrs. Christian de Guigné III), Gift of Ronna and
Eric Hoffman.

1. Afternoon Dress, Aladdin
Christian Dior, winter 1947
Full-skirted wrap dress of gold silk grosgrain with self-satin stripe, brown alligator belt. Bias-cut skirt is gathered and pleated into a short waist seam in back only, cut in one with the bodice in front. Dior, who named each season's collection, called this the Corolle line. The American press came up with the name by which it is known today — the New Look.
Gift of Mrs. Eloise Heidland
1982.18.3a-b

2. Afternoon Dress
Cristobal Balenciaga, winter 1947
Bustle-back dress of black silk bengaline with slim underskirt ruched at the sides to form graceful horizontal folds. The overskirt is stitched to the underskirt across the front, forming a short, puffy peplum extending nearly to the hem at back. It is looped up into graduated folds at the center back and trimmed with a black velvet bow.
Gift of Mrs. Eloise Heidland
1982.18.1
Hat gift of Mr. E. J. Larson

3. Afternoon Dress
Jeanne Lanvin, winter 1947
Double-breasted dress of navy wool crepe, the hips emphasized with a gathered swag of fabric draped across the back. Its slender lines and square shoulders continue the pre–New Look silhouette.
Lent by Lillian B. Schuman

4. Evening Dress
Pierre Balmain, winter 1947
Long, slim gown of chocolate brown silk bengaline, the ruched bodice bloused over a boned foundation. The double skirt is also ruched along the center back, giving a bustle effect.
Gift of Mrs. Eloise Heidland
1982.18.2

5. Evening Dress
Pierre Balmain, probably winter 1947
Strapless gown of white silk tulle. Silver sequins and silvered glass bead loops encrust the bodice and are sprinkled over the three-layer skirt. According to the donor, Balmain was asked one evening at a dinner party to design a dress for her. He promptly sketched this dress on the tablecloth.
Gift of Lillian B. Schuman
1986.106.1

6. Afternoon Ensemble
Christian Dior, spring 1948
Shirtwaist and multilayered full skirt of black silk faille. The underskirt of faille and silk tulle supports a skirt formed from a single length of fabric, narrowing towards the ends, that folds back and forth upon itself. From the Zig Zag collection.
Gift of Mrs. Eloise Heidland
1982.18.4a-b
Hat gift of Mr. E. J. Larson
1984.24.5

7. Cocktail Dress
Christian Dior, probably winter 1948
Cap-sleeved blouse and full, calf-length skirt of black silk velvet embroidered with radiating bands of iridescent faceted blue glass beads. The neckline, which turns down to a small velvet collar, plunges daringly to a high waistband of unembroidered velvet. Matching beaded skull cap.
Bequest of Jeanne Magnin
1987.25.1a-d

8. Short Evening Dress
Christian Dior, winter 1948
Strapless black silk velvet bodice and black silk faille skirt stiffened with horsehair and silk tulle. Matching silk velvet cummerbund. Skirt falls in numerous umbrella-like folds from a slightly dropped waistline and is supported by a separate boned tulle petticoat. From the Ailée collection.
Bequest of Jeanne Magnin
1987.25.2a-b
Hat gift of Mr. E. J. Larson

9. Ballgown, Cygne Noir
Christian Dior, winter 1949
Strapless bodice and skirt of black silk satin and velvet with black silk velvet stole. The dress is from the Milieu du Siècle collection and has its characteristic small, criss-crossed bodice and full skirt. An enormous velvet bow with trailing ends incorporated into the skirt creates the asymmetrical hemline, which dips lower on the left side.
Gift of Mrs. Leslie Roos
1979.51.15a-c

10. Ballgown, Junon
Christian Dior, winter 1949
Bodice and skirt of white silk tulle embroidered with blue, silver, copper, purple, green, and iridescent sequins, over pale aqua silk faille. "Junon" represents the first of the Three Graces. The tiny strapless bodice is dwarfed by a huge skirt of graduated, horsehair-lined tulle petals supported by an underskirt stiffened with horsehair and silk net. An original sample of the embroidery, by Rébé, is preserved at the Musée des Arts de la Mode in Paris. From the Milieu du Siècle collection.
Gift of I. Magnin & Co.
49.25.2a-b

11. Ballgown, Venus
Christian Dior, winter 1949
Bodice and skirt of pale pink silk tulle embroidered with iridescent pink feather-shaped paillettes, iridescent and silver sequins, pearls, and rhinestones over pale pink silk and silk tulle. Matching sash. The shape of each petal is influenced by the curved paillettes. Embroidery by Rébé. "Venus" represents the second of the Three Graces; the third, "Diana," is in the collection of the Los Angeles County Museum of Art. From the Milieu du Siècle collection.
Gift of I. Magnin & Co.
49.25.1a-c

12. Suit
Christian Dior, probably spring 1950
Skirt and jacket of heavy black wool gabardine. The jacket shows the apogee of the peplum. From the Vertical Line collection.
Gift of Mrs. Clarence E. Knapp
1988.46a-b

13. Evening Dress
Pierre Balmain, ca. 1950
Strapless gown of pink silk faille embroidered with pearl beads, rhinestones, and silver bullion, matching pearl-edged underskirt. Commercial buyers were charged admission to couture collection showings, the price being equivalent to the cost of a dress. This dress was the "admission ticket" from a Balmain collection.
Gift of Lillian B. Schuman
1986.106.2a-b

14. Dance Dress
Pierre Balmain, spring 1952
Strapless, short evening dress of pearl-gray silk organza studded with rhinestones. The pleated bust detail extends to small "wings" in back. The full skirt is composed of individual cut petals, some embroidered with white sequins, scattered with pendant rhinestone teardrops. From the Lys de France collection.
Gift of Lillian B. Schuman
1986.106.3

15. Evening Dress
Christian Dior, winter 1952
Halter-neck bodice, calf-length dirndl-style skirt and short jacket of heavy cream silk ottoman, with matching belt. The snug jacket is cut from only two pieces of silk, its short sleeves formed by underarm gussets. From the Profilée collection.
Bequest of Jeanne Magnin
1987.25.15a-d

16. Evening Dress, Anet
Pierre Balmain, spring 1953
Full-skirted, strapless gown of white silk tulle trimmed with horizontal rows of machine lace, pink silk satin underbodice and draped sash. The skirt is supported on many-layered tulle petticoats. Worn by the donor to her senior dance.
Gift of Cynthia Schuman
1986.106.4

17. Suit
Cristobal Balenciaga, winter 1954
Jacket and skirt of black, gray, and white-flecked wool tweed. The jacket's large cape collar fastens with black suede ties.
1985.44.195a-b

18. Suit
Cristobal Balenciaga, winter 1954
Fitted jacket and slender skirt of heavy black, white, and gray wool tweed. The jacket's side front dart seams stop short of its hem, enabling it to fit snugly over the hips. Broad collar and flapped breast pockets add a military flavor.
Gift of Mrs. Leslie Roos
1979.51.25a-b

19. Evening Dress
Christian Dior, winter 1954
Long princess-line gown of burgundy and gold silk
"Persian" brocade over separate silk tulle petticoats.
Matching shoes. From the H-Line collection.
Bequest of Jeanne Magnin
1987.25.8a-b
Shoes, 1987.25.9a-b

20. Evening Dress, Grand Première
Pierre Balmain, winter 1955
Long black silk velvet sheath trimmed with self-bows.
To form each bow the velvet was slashed and gathered
into a separate bow knot and loops, and a rectangle of
black silk faille slipped behind. This was a model,
purchased by the donor at the couture salon at
I. Magnin & Co. in San Francisco
Gift of Mrs. Mary Ritter
1986.105.12
Shoes gift of Mrs. Leslie Roos
1979.51.97

21. Evening Dress
Christian Dior, winter 1955, designed by
Yves Saint Laurent
Fitted long-sleeved gown of black silk velvet with
oyster-white satin "obi" with trailing ends. This is the
first dress Yves Saint Laurent designed while at the
house of Dior, immortalized by the Richard Avedon
photo of Dovima posed before elephants at the Cirque
d'Hiver. The trailing sash has been shortened.
The Eleanor Christenson de Guigné Collection
Gift of Ronna and Eric Hoffman in honor of
Ian McKibbin White
1987.12
Matching shoes, 1985.44.529a-b

22. Evening Dress, Soirée Fleurie
Christian Dior, winter 1955
Cap-sleeved bodice, full skirt and sash of white silk
satin embroidered with silver and silver-gilt strip,
polychrome stones, and iridescent white and gilt
loops. As with some of Dior's earlier dresses, Soirée
Fleurie has an eighteenth-century inspiration, which is
centered in the embroidery.
Bequest of Jeanne Magnin
1987.25.4a-c
Shoes, 1985.44.579a-b

23. Evening Dress
Madame Grès, ca. 1952–1955
One-shoulder dress of ice-blue silk jersey. The firmly
set pleats of the bodice contrast with the open pleats of
the skirt, which drape gracefully to an asymmetrical
hem. Madame Grès is celebrated for this type of
timeless, sculptural design, usually executed in her
preferred fabric, silk jersey.
Lent by Lillian B. Schuman

24. Afternoon Ensemble
Christian Dior, winter 1956
Two-piece dress and jacket of black and white wool
tweed. The bodice has knitted black wool short sleeves
and is fastened to the skirt with snaps around the waist.
From the Aimant collection
1985.44.3a-c
Hat gift of Mr. E. J. Larson

25. Dinner Dress
Christian Dior, winter 1956
Long-sleeved bodice and full skirt of black silk faille.
The décolletage is supported both by wired shoulders
and a long boned underbodice of the type commonly
known as a merry widow. The skirt of this dress,
buoyed by innumerable attached tulle petticoats, will
stand by itself.
Gift of Mrs. Leslie Roos
1979.51.14a-b
Hat gift of Catherine B. Halpern
1984.15

26. Short Evening Dress
Attributed to Chanel, ca. 1956
Slim, strapless dress of black silk crepe chiffon over
black silk, with self-cord belt and attached flowing
shoulder scarf. The dress is fitted to its boned
underdress with deep vertical pleats that release to
form a flared hem.
Gift of Mrs. Leslie Roos
1979.51.2

27. Evening Dress
Cristobal Balenciaga, winter 1957
Strapless short dress of red, black, and fuchsia warp-
printed silk ottoman, dominated by a bouffant puff-ball
skirt.
Lent by Cynthia Schuman

28. Day Dress
Christian Dior, spring 1958, designed by
Yves Saint Laurent
"Sack-back" dress of black, gray, and white printed
silk, matching picture hat. From the Trapeze collection, the first designed by Yves Saint Laurent after
the death of Christian Dior. Trapeze dresses appear to
swing freely from the shoulders, hence the name.
1985.44.456a-c
Hat, 1985.44.351

29. Day Ensemble
Christian Dior, spring 1958, designed by
Yves Saint Laurent
Two-piece dress and short jacket of black and silver-
gray silk herringbone tweed. A subtler version of the
trapeze line.
1985.44.7a-c

30. Short Evening Dress
Christian Dior, spring 1958, designed by
Yves Saint Laurent
Strapless dress of cherry-red silk faille, underbodice
with toning pink silk net petticoats. This strapless
version of the trapeze theme has a fluid drape built on
the customary firm foundation—a boned underbodice
with attached underskirts. Matching stole, not shown.
1985.44.120a

31. Cocktail Dress
Cristobal Balenciaga, 1958
Dress of royal blue silk shantung, matching belt. The
dress is shaped to the waist with a curved horizontal
dart at center back and set off with a floating panel
attached across the neckline and shoulders. Matching
shoes.
1985.44.305a-b
Shoes, 1985.44.555a-b
Hat gift of Mr. E. J. Larson
1984.24.64

32. Dance Dress, Sucre d'Orge
Maggy Rouff, ca. 1958–1959
Strapless short evening dress of self-embroidered white
silk organdy, the skirt formed by three double-
scalloped flounces underlined with a fringed layer of
shocking chartreuse silk taffeta. Leather-backed belt
with oversized bow of chartreuse silk taffeta. The skirt
dips slightly in back and is supported on an immense
chartreuse net petticoat.
Lent by Mrs. John N. Rosekrans, Jr.

33. Suit
Christian Dior, winter 1959, designed by
Yves Saint Laurent
Skirt, jacket, and belt of green and brown wool plaid,
cap-sleeved blouse of green wool jersey. The boxy,
double-breasted jacket balances a full, double-box-
pleated skirt.
The Eleanor Christenson de Guigné Collection
Skirt, jacket, and belt lent by Ronna Hoffman
1985.44.196

34. Evening Suit
Christian Dior, winter 1959, designed by
Yves Saint Laurent
Short cocktail dress of black brushed wool, tulip-
shaped skirt, black silk satin shoulder straps.
Matching double-breasted jacket, the revers of the
portrait neckline of black silk satin. Black silk satin
and velvet "artichoke" hat.
1985.44.2a-b
Hat, 1985.44.322

35. Suit
Christian Dior, spring 1960, designed by
Yves Saint Laurent
Cardigan jacket and skirt of gray and white
houndstooth check wool twill, the skirt shaped with
five pinch pleats at each hip. This spring collection by
Saint Laurent was considered too youthful by the house
of Dior for its established clientele and eventually led
Saint Laurent to form his own couture house.
1985.44.304a-c
Shoes, 1985.44.533a-b

36. Wedding Dress
Hubert de Givenchy, spring 1960
Short-sleeved, high-waisted dress of ivory silk satin,
extending to a majestic rounded train. Matching cap
and attached tulle veil appliquéd with curved silk satin
petals. (Veil reproduced from original.)
Gift of Mrs. Vincent M. Hughes
1989.11.1-2

37. Suit
Chanel, ca. 1960
Jacket and skirt of pink angora wool twill, multicolored
chiné-printed silk taffeta blouse with self-tie at neck.
The same silk trims the jacket and skirt.
The Eleanor Christenson de Guigné Collection
Lent by Ronna Hoffman
Handbag gift of Mrs. Leslie Roos
1981.79.4

38. Evening Dress
Christian Dior, spring 1961, designed by Marc Bohan
Long gown with appliquéd bodice of oversized, exotic
flowers of pale chartreuse guipure and circular skirt of
chartreuse silk organza over layers of yellow silk
chiffon and stiffened shantung.
1985.44.445

39. Suit
Chanel, spring 1963
Jacket and slim "apron" skirt of ivory raw silk, match-
ing blouse of china silk. The skirt's layered effect is
repeated on the jacket's collar, revers, pockets,
and cuffs.
The Eleanor Christenson de Guigné Collection
Lent by Ronna Hoffman
Shoes, 1985.44.596a-b

40. Evening Ensemble
Cristobal Balenciaga, spring 1963
Long dress and jacket of cream silk faille with floral
cutwork and embroidery in orange and green silk floss
and silver thread and sequins. The dress was originally
shown with a long, capelike evening wrap instead of the
jacket.
Bequest of Jeanne Magnin
1987.25.5a-b
Shoes bequest of Jeanne Magnin
1987.31.37a-b

41. Sport Ensemble
Cristobal Balenciaga, winter 1963
Pleated skirt, short jacket, and caped cloak of brown
and beige wool plaid. The jacket sleeves, when slipped
through the cloak's armholes, give it the appearance of
a caped coat.
The Eleanor Christenson de Guigné Collection
Lent by Ronna Hoffman

42. Evening Dress
Cristobal Balenciaga, winter 1963
Sari-style gown of hot pink silk cloqué edged with
pink, purple, and silver sequins, the back extending
like a train to drape across the front and over the right
shoulder. Unlike a traditional sari, the bodice is
attached to a boned foundation. This dress carries the
label of Balenciaga's Spanish branch, Eisa.
Lent by Mrs. John N. Rosekrans, Jr.

43. At-home Ensemble
Madame Grès, winter 1964
"Harem" outfit of heavy white silk with floral brocade
in blue, red, and gold. It is a kite-shaped bag of two
pieces of bias-cut brocade, with openings for arms,
legs, and head. *Vogue* termed it "the Dalai Lama robe."
1985.44.12

44. Theater Suit
Yves Saint Laurent, winter 1964
Sleeveless tunic, straight skirt, and jacket of ivory and
gold silk brocade, the jacket trimmed with white mink.
1985.44.266a-c

45. Evening Dress
Yves Saint Laurent, winter 1964
Sleeveless, princess-line gown of pale pink silk faille
embroidered with strawberry, orange, and rust silk,
silver thread, rhinestones, and bugle beads. The
neckline and hem are edged with red and white
rhinestones and silver thread. This was the original
model, purchased in Paris.
1985.44.180
Shoes, 1985.44.594a-b

46. Suit
Chanel, ca. 1964
Skirt and jacket of green, orange, and pale and hot pink tweed edged with matching braid. Matching printed silk shorts with tweed trim, and blouse of acid green slub silk. The orange and green yarns in this unusual tweed are held in place by horizontal rows of chain stitching. The jacket is trimmed with Chanel's trademark buttons.
Gift of Mrs. John N. Rosekrans, Jr.
1983.36.49a-d

47. Evening Dress
Cristobal Balenciaga, spring 1965
Long dress of red silk satin. It is cut in only two pieces, seamed at center front and back and extending from the front to form the short sleeves and trailing back neckline tie.
Gift of Mrs. Adele Simpson
1982.91.11

48. Suit
Cristobal Balenciaga, winter 1965
Double-breasted, fitted jacket and flared skirt of bright yellow silk doubleknit. The skirt's exaggerated silhouette is enhanced by wide front and back box pleats.
1985.44.35a-c
Hat gift of Mrs. Leslie Roos
1979.51.148
Shoes, 1985.44.509a-b

49. Evening Dress
Madame Grès, winter 1965
Ankle-length tent dress of blue-gray silk zibeline embroidered center front and back with faceted silver, pearl, and crystal beads, silver paillettes and ribbon and clear prisms, and at the hem with silver lace, rhinestones, and colored prisms. Though the front and back of the dress are identical in cut, on the body it forms a free-falling sack-back.
The Eleanor Christenson de Guigné Collection
Lent by Ronna Hoffman
Shoes, 1985.44.594

50. Day Dress
Madame Grès, ca. 1964–1965
Bias-cut dress of beige angora jersey, self-cord belt. Beneath the belt the waist of the dress is partly gathered—from center front to center back on the right side only. The draped skirt wraps across the back.
1985.44.225a-b

51. Pantsuit
André Courrèges, ca. 1965
Short tunic and slightly flared trousers of bright red-orange wool doubleknit, welted seams. The patch pockets are non-functioning.
Gift of Mrs. Mary Ritter
1986.105.11a-b

52. At-home Ensemble
Madame Grès, ca. 1965
Blouse of black silk zibeline, the wide cape collar of two overlapping semicircles, orange silk zibeline palazzo pants. This ensemble, with masterly cut, presents the figure as simple geometric shapes.
1985.44.43a-b
Shoes, 1985.44.515a-b

53. Suit
Cristobal Balenciaga, spring 1966
Jacket and skirt of black, white, and camel double-cloth wool twill, black silk shantung sleeveless blouse. This bias-cut suit is exemplary of Balenciaga's mastery over fabric. The jacket is made in only three main pieces, with seams along the shoulder and sides. The skirt, falling from a wide yoke, is made from one piece of wool; the joining seam runs diagonally across the back from the left waist to the right knee and has a small triangular gusset inserted at center back hem.
1985.44.31a-c
Shoes, 1985.44.499a-b

54. Evening Dress
Cristobal Balenciaga, spring 1966
Strapless dress of black silk gazar with boned underbodice; pink silk gazar bolero not shown.
1985.44.214a
Shoes, 1985.44.534a-b

55. Cocktail Dress
Cristobal Balenciaga, winter 1966
Sleeveless A-line dress of magenta slub silk. Boned
black silk underdress trimmed with machine lace.
Demure in front, the neckline plunges well below the
waist in back, revealing a lacy petticoat.
1985.44.429a-b
Hat gift of Mr. E. J. Larson
1984.24.46
Shoes, 1985.44.519a-b

56. Cocktail Dress
Cristobal Balenciaga, winter 1966
Dress of fuchsia silk crepe. It is another example of
virtuoso cut, made primarily from a single piece of silk
and shaped with darts at the yoke. The sleeves are
pieced at the elbow.
Gift of Mrs. Adele Simpson
1982.91.10

57. Evening Dress
Christian Dior, winter 1966, designed by Marc Bohan
Short dress of machine Chantilly lace, the flared,
pendant sleeves trimmed with black satin ribbon bows.
Strapless underdress of black silk chiffon and satin.
1985.44.17a-b

58. Dance Dress
Pierre Cardin, ca. 1966
Halter mini-dress of doublefaced white wool crepe with
hem and neckline straps of padded self-tubing.
Lent by Ronna Hoffman

59. Dance Dress
Yves Saint Laurent, spring 1967
African-inspired mini-dress of beige silk organza,
natural wooden beads and raffia.
Lent by Mrs. John N. Rosekrans, Jr.

60. Après-ski Ensemble
Cristobal Balenciaga, winter 1967
Pointed tunic of oversized brown and white
houndstooth-check printed wool jersey, trousers
of corded white wool doublecloth.
1985.44.58a-c
Hat gift of Mrs. Leslie Roos
1979.51.151

61. Casual Ensemble
Cristobal Balenciaga, winter 1967
Jacket and culottes of pink and cream double-weave
wool twill. Different faces of the same fabric are used
to make cream-colored culottes and pink jacket.
Balenciaga originally showed the top as a vest;
however, it was ordered as a jacket.
1985.44.18a-b
Shoes, 1985.44.513a-b
Hat gift of Mrs. Leslie Roos
1979.51.126

62. At-home Ensemble
Madame Grès, winter 1967
"Harem" outfit of silk with a psychedelic warp-print in
aqua, yellow, pink, brown, and purple and a supplementary gold and white floral brocade. It is essentially
an elaborate wrap-around, with a side slit forming the
right trouser leg.
1985.44.11
Sandals, 1985.44.592a-b

63. Evening Dress
Cristobal Balenciaga, winter 1967
Long, sleeveless gown of bright yellow silk crepe, the
uneven hemline trimmed with matching ostrich
feathers. Detachable, feather-trimmed shoulder cape
hides a deep V-neckline in back.
1985.44.185a-b

64. Afternoon Ensemble
Yves Saint Laurent, spring 1968
Long tunic and skirt of daisy-patterned orange, white, and yellow cotton guipure over sheer orange silk.
1985.44.290a-b

65. Evening Dress
Cristobal Balenciaga, spring 1968
White reembroidered cotton lace tunic over dress of caramel silk crepe and sheer, pleated silk organza. Black silk satin ribbon trim. From Balenciaga's last collection.
1985.44.288
Shoes, 1985.44.507a-b

66. Coat
Hubert de Givenchy, winter 1968
Three-quarter-length coat of camel-colored wool rattine with black silk velvet collar. The raglan sleeves form a curved yoke that echoes the coat's gently curved silhouette.
1985.44.216

67. Pantsuit
Yves Saint Laurent, winter 1968
Tunic and trousers of persimmon wool doubleknit, matching silk crepe underbodice with attached red-orange knit sequinned sleeves. This ensemble also came with a skirt.
1985.44.106a-c
Shoes, 1985.44.503a-b

68. Evening Ensemble
Hubert de Givenchy, winter 1968
Jumpsuit of purple silk gazar with patch pockets, turquoise silk satin ribbon sash. The wearer had the option of wearing the sash shown or a purple one.
1985.44.182a-b

69. Hostess Ensemble
Hubert de Givenchy, winter 1968
Dolman-sleeved blouse and slim trousers of black silk satin, calf-length overskirt of black silk with overall floral embroidery in polychrome silk floss, yarn, metallic thread, and crimped sequins. Black satin ribbon belt.
1985.44.50a-b
Skirt lent by Ronna Hoffman
Shoes, 1985.44.509a-b

70. Evening Dress
Hubert de Givenchy, winter 1968
Dress of brown silk crepe embroidered with stripped and trimmed brown and white ostrich feathers, worn over underdress of brown silk with a wide black silk velvet border at hem. Black satin ribbon sash.
1985.44.121a-c
Shoes, 1985.44.524

71. Dance Dress
Yves Saint Laurent, winter 1968
Sleeveless mini-dress of black suede embroidered with coral and green stones and glass beads, and gold wire. Attached suede fringe at hem.
Gift of Mrs. Thomas Kempner
1986.99.40

72. Sport Ensemble
Madame Grès, ca. 1965–1968
Coat and trousers of wool twill doublecloth, the outer face camel-colored, the inner face of red, cream, and green brushed plaid. Matching plaid blouse and stole, tan leather belt.
The Eleanor Christenson de Guigné Collection
Lent by Ronna Hoffman

73. Evening Dress
Madame Grès, ca. 1965–1968
One-shoulder floor-length gown of royal blue silk crepe, the skirt slit thigh-high at right front and back. The asymmetrical hipband seams parallel the neckline.
Gift of Mrs. Adele Simpson
1982.91.19

74. Pantsuit
Yves Saint Laurent, spring 1969
Safari suit of khaki-brown wool gabardine, with leather-tipped self-belt.
Gift of Mrs. Thomas Kempner
1986.99.5a-c

75. Sport Ensemble
Hubert de Givenchy, winter 1969
Double-breasted coat and narrow trousers of wool and silk stretch knit, printed with leopard pattern in shades of brown and beige.
The Eleanor Christenson de Guigné Collection
Lent by Ronna Hoffman

76. Greatcoat
Yves Saint Laurent, winter 1969
Full-skirted, caped maxi-overcoat of loden green wool flecked with white.
Gift of Mrs. Thomas Kempner
1986.99.17

77. Lounging Pajamas
Attributed to Chanel, ca. 1969
Tunic and trousers of sheer red silk voile with floral patterns printed in blue and woven in gold thread, gold braid trim. A deep red silk lining lends a purplish cast to the blue flowers.
The Eleanor Christenson de Guigné Collection
Lent by Ronna Hoffman
Shoes, 1985.44.557a-b

78. Daytime Ensemble
Yves Saint Laurent, 1970
Cavalier midi-coat of colored silk velvet patchwork, blouse of aubergine wool gauze, skirt of black wool crepe, and boots of studded brown suede. The coat's lining is also patchwork, in different shades of gray silk taffeta, to correspond to the velvet shell.
Gift of Mrs. Thomas Kempner
1986.99.16a-d

79. Coat
Yves Saint Laurent, spring 1971
Mini-coat of turquoise fox. Part of the Forties collection, which received universally negative press. Yves Saint Laurent was accused of degrading women and elevating bad taste, and it was predicted that his career would soon be over. Retro looks eventually infiltrated all levels of fashion.
Lent by Mrs. John N. Rosekrans, Jr.

80. Evening Dress
Yves Saint Laurent, winter 1971
Short dress of sheer taupe silk chiffon with flared, bias-cut skirt, self-tie at neck and self-belt with rhinestone buckle. Matching underdress. The design of this soft dress shows a thirties influence.
Gift of Mrs. Thomas Kempner
1986.99.43a-c

81. Sport Ensemble
Madame Grès, ca. 1971
Dolman-sleeved blouse with waist tie, hot pants, and circular wrap skirt of off-white wool jersey. The blouse sleeves, which appear to be pieced, are of a single piece of jersey wrapped under the arm and stitched to itself. This ensemble also has matching flared trousers.
1985.44.206a-c

82. Playsuit and Domino
Madame Grès, ca. 1971
One-sleeved hot-pants jumpsuit of black silk velvet, black silk taffeta domino.
1985.44.317a-b

83. Opera Ensemble
Christian Dior, ca. 1972, designed by Marc Bohan
Floor-length cape and skirt of midnight blue silk and viscose velvet. Blouse and bow-trimmed sash of blue-gray ombré silk chiffon, matching collar of dyed ostrich feathers.
Gift of Mrs. Thomas Kempner
1986.99.38a-e

84. Evening Dress
Madame Grès, ca. 1974
Full, gathered blouse with asymmetrical neckline over a long, narrow skirt, of charcoal-gray silk faille. This is a version of the style of dress that Madame Grès designed for herself and often wore.
1985.44.200a-b
Shoes, 1985.44.539

85. Evening Dress and Coat
Madame Grès, ca. 1974
Dress and circular coat of purple and green silk paper taffeta. The bodice of the dress, invisible beneath the wide coat, is of pieced purple and green taffeta.
1985.44.446a-b
Shoes, 1985.44.556a-b

86. At-home Ensemble
Madame Grès, 1976
Red, white, and blue striped silk crepe, blue silk taffeta belt. This deceptively simple garment is half dress, half trousers.
1985.44.202a-b

87. Evening Ensemble
Yves Saint Laurent, spring 1977
Peasant blouse of paisley-printed petrol-blue silk chiffon. Ruffled chiffon stole printed with a larger-scale paisley pattern. Full skirt of matching paisley-printed chiné silk taffeta. Ruffled underskirt of ultramarine silk taffeta, brown satin ribbon sash. In 1976 and 1977, Yves Saint Laurent introduced collections based on rich peasant and gypsy costumes.
The Eleanor Christenson de Guigné Collection
Lent by Ronna Hoffman

88. Evening Ensemble
Yves Saint Laurent, spring 1977
Peasant blouse of purple silk chiffon shot with gold. Silk-fringed stole of purple and gold silk chiffon. Full skirt of purple silk moiré banded with bordeaux velvet. Ruffled underskirt of wine-red silk taffeta. Bordeaux satin ribbon sash.
The Eleanor Christenson de Guigné Collection
Lent by Ronna Hoffman

89. Evening Ensemble
Emanuel Ungaro, spring 1977
Kimono and sash of lightweight ivory silk printed with black stripes, lined in Chinese rhomboid-patterned ivory silk, edged with silk-satin ribbon and silk braid. Underskirt of plain ivory silk, the hem bordered with woven stripes in gilt and black thread.
Gift of Mrs. Thomas Kempner
1986.99.27a-c
Shoes, 1985.44.580a-b

90. Evening Pajamas
Yves Saint Laurent, winter 1977
Double-sleeved slit tunic of black and polychrome printed silk crepe trimmed with black silk soutache and tassels, matching silk-fringed sash. Trousers of turquoise plain silk figured with satin spots. From the Chinese collection.
Gift of Mrs. Thomas Kempner
1986.99.33a-c

91. Pantsuit
Yves Saint Laurent, 1977
Smock jacket and trousers of oatmeal cashmere, high-necked ruffled blouse of cream satin-striped silk crepe.
Gift of Mrs. Thomas Kempner
1986.99.9a-b

92. Evening Dress
Madame Grès, ca. 1977
Slim, floor-length dress of forest green silk taffeta with a halter top and a short, puffed bias-cut overskirt tightly gathered into a dropped waistband. Matching bias-cut puffed cape/collar.
The Eleanor Christenson de Guigné Collection
Lent by Ronna Hoffman
Shoes, 1985.44.565a-b

93. Cocktail Dress
Hubert de Givenchy, winter 1978
Strapless black velvet sheath with yoke and long sleeves of rhinestone-studded sheer black silk crepe georgette.
Gift of Mrs. Thomas Kempner
1986.99.34

94. Suit
Yves Saint Laurent, winter 1979
Jacket and skirt of wide-ribbed white wool twill with revers, cuffs, and skirt panels of black silk velvet. Long-sleeved black silk-satin blouse. From Saint Laurent's Picasso collection. The suit's cubist effect is achieved by strong black and white patterning.
Gift of Mrs. Thomas Kempner
1986.99.14a-b

95. Evening Dress
Madame Grès, 1979
Long, halter-neck gown of draped forest green silk jersey with detachable draped bib collar of celadon silk jersey. This was the original model.
Museum purchase, Gift of Eleanore Stalker Foster, Julia Geist, Suzanne Reger, and anonymous donors
1988.17

96. Evening Dress
Madame Grès, ca. 1980
Full-skirted, gathered evening dress of maroon silk paper taffeta, matching wide belt. Its petticoat has a wide hem of matching taffeta.
1985.44.119a-c
Shoes, 1985.44.546a-b

97. Suit
Yves Saint Laurent, winter 1981
Red wool jacket with black silk velvet revers and cuffs, fuchsia silk-satin blouse with falling jabot, black wool *grain de poudre* skirt. The mixing of strong, clashing colors, pioneered by Yves Saint Laurent, has become standard practice in current fashion.
The Eleanor Christenson de Guigné Collection
Jacket lent by Ronna Hoffman
1985.44.435

98. Trouser Suit
Yves Saint Laurent, spring 1982
"Spencer" and trousers of navy wool gabardine, matching silk jersey blouse.
The Eleanor Christenson de Guigné Collection
Lent by Ronna Hoffman

99. Afternoon Dress
Yves Saint Laurent, winter 1982
Slim dress of spotted silk crepe with fantasy leopard print in gray, green, blue, purple, and brown. Large scarf of matching printed silk chiffon. A wrap effect is given by a supplementary bodice front attached at the right side that stretches across to fasten at the left shoulder, and a double ruffle up the left side of the skirt. The broadening of the shoulder line is highlighted by a double flounce encircling each sleeve.
The Eleanor Christenson de Guigné Collection
Lent by Ronna Hoffman

100. Evening Dress

Yves Saint Laurent, winter 1982
Long, gored gown of midnight blue velvet with gigot sleeves and bandeau of jonquil silk slipper-satin.
The Eleanor Christenson de Guigné Collection
Lent by Ronna Hoffman

101. Day Ensemble

Yves Saint Laurent, spring 1983
Double-breasted coat dress of gray wool twill with white pinstripe.
Gift of Mrs. Thomas Kempner
1986.99.15

102. Afternoon Suit

Hubert de Givenchy, winter 1987
Jacket and skirt of red- and black-printed yellow silk faille with cuffs and revers of black silk velvet, fastening with a single faceted amber button. Oversized black silk velvet beret "Basque" trimmed with red silk faille bow. The motif for the print of this suit, Reine Margot, was borrowed from the designs of Christian Bérard, to whom this collection was dedicated.
Gift of Maison Givenchy, 1989

103. Evening Dress, Columba

Christian Lacroix, winter 1987
Commedia-inspired dress with black silk velvet bodice and puffed sleeves, the yoke formed of a latticework of velvet ribbon. Short, full black silk taffeta skirt striped with black velvet. Black silk velvet bicorne trimmed with bows and a black satin rose. From the first collection Christian Lacroix presented under his own label, in July 1987.
Gift of Maison Lacroix, 1989

104. Evening Dress

Yves Saint Laurent, winter 1987
Mini-dress of chocolate brown silk applied with brown and white stripped ostrich feathers, black silk ribbon trim. This dress was strapless in its original design, the shoulder straps added at the request of the client.
Gift of Yves Saint Laurent in memory of Claudia de Osborne
1988.16

105. Evening Dress

Madame Grès, spring 1988
Bubble-back sleeveless sheath of polychrome, paisley-printed chiné silk taffeta. Madame Grès's exquisitely draped version of the pouf, a theme she interpreted many times during her long career. Technically our retrospective is finished in 1987, but out of respect for the great talents of Madame Grès and her enormous contributions to haute couture it seems fitting to include a dress from her last collection. Madame Grès was forced to close the doors of her *maison* in April 1988.
Gift of Maison Grès, 1989

BALENCIAGA
AND SPAIN

Marie Andrée Jouve

Balenciaga, winter 1947

If the Spanish Civil War of 1936 had not occurred, perhaps Balenciaga never would have come to Paris.

The question to ask after that is, "Would his work have been as impregnated with Spanishness if he had never left his country?" He was born there, he died there, and there he created three flourishing houses: in San Sebastián, in Madrid, and in Barcelona, all with a most select clientele. During the twenties, he dressed the Spanish royal family, who often passed the summers at their palace in San Sebastián, at the same time that Chanel had installed herself across the border at Biarritz.

Balenciaga adored the Pays Basque, where he was born in 1895, and manifested in his personal character the severity, reserve, and natural distinction of his beloved country. Much later he constructed a house at Igueldo, superbly situated, dominating the sea and the Basque coast, where he would go frequently to rest between his Paris collections. He had always wanted to build another home near Valencia, where, in fact, he met his death in 1972.

When the Civil War exploded in 1936, he was forced to close his Spanish couture houses and took refuge in London, where at that moment the celebrated Worth reigned in the world of fashion. He presented himself at the House of Worth to find employment in one of the ateliers, but Worth, who knew the great reputation of Balenciaga in Spain, refused to engage him. Cristobal Balenciaga, offended and desperate, replied, "But Mr. Worth, I know how to sew." It was true that he knew all aspects of construction and could do all with his own hands—to the great admiration of his collaborators—and rival couturiers. After presenting himself for work at Maggy Rouff, also without success, he left London for good and arrived in Paris where he rediscovered his Basque friends, refugees like himself, who offered to help him. In a cafe on the Champs Elysées in the winter of 1937, he decided to open a *maison de haute couture* at 10, avenue Georges V, where during the next thirty years, Balenciaga reigned as the leader of French fashion. Throughout these years in Paris, he continued to think of Spain. After the termination of the Civil War, he reopened his three Spanish houses one after another at one-year intervals.

He brought with him to Paris the inspiration of his country, as evidenced in his Infanta dresses of 1939, and his audacious mixtures of brown (in all shades of the Spanish

earth) and black worked with heavy embroideries of passementerie and jet on gowns and toreador-inspired boleros of the
forties. His style and technique, already impressive, were
marked with an absolute classicism that became the frame-
work for all his future creations.

The grace, elegance, and refinement of the clothes
of Balenciaga during the fifties, in black and with the trans-
parency of lace, sometimes softened by pink, took inspiration
from the popular *majas* of Goya with their mysterious *tapadas*
(veiled headpieces, which encircled and sometimes hid the
face).

The constant search for simplicity and the paring
away of detail reached its apogee during the sixties. Severity,
volume, abstraction, and a dazzling technique were manifested in fabrics that were painstakingly realized, rich, and
sometimes strange and unusual in conception. One finds the
influence of Zurbarán in certain dresses of the early sixties
that are constructed in heavy and sumptuous textiles. In the
last collections, an evening or bridal gown in stiff fabric cut in
a flaring trapeze line evokes a Spanish madonna, hieratic like
a statue, spiritual and radiant.

The influence of popular costume is equally
remarkable, especially in his very original headpieces and
hats, in the form and length of certain skirts, the huge variety
of capes, and in the many embroidery techniques inspired by
certain provinces (Salamanca) or materials and color (shawls
of Manila).

Balenciaga loved to spend hours in the Prado and to
walk along La Concha, the beach at San Sebastián. He had
many dear friends in Spain, like the painter Zuloaga. One of
them, who knew him well, felt that he was obsessed by the
ideal of perfection. In Paris, he wrote all his notes to his ateliers in Spanish, usually translated into French by his sec-
retary, and he always lost his temper in his native language.
His early years in Spain were the search and formation of style
and technique from which he brought us his amazing
"souplesse construite." His years in France were the search and
formation of perfection, elegance, and harmony of proportion.
One could apply to Balenciaga this axiom, which is, in fact, a
conclusion:

> *Architecte pour les plans*
> *Sculpteur pour la forme*
> *Peintre pour la couleur*
> *Musicien pour l'harmonie*
> *Philosophe pour la mesure.*

*Marie Andrée Jouve is Curator of the Balenciaga Archives,
Paris.*

Balenciaga, winter 1955

Balenciaga, spring 1967

BIOGRAPHICAL NOTES ON THE COUTURIERS

Caroline Rennolds Milbank

Cristobal Balenciaga

In her novel *October Blood*, Francine du Plessix Gray described her narrator's mother, a woman who lived for elegance: "To say that Mother was fussy about clothes is like saying Queen Victoria was conscious of etiquette." The picture of one of fiction's most chic women is further clarified by the mention that she dressed only in Balenciaga, and only in one of his chemise dresses at that: beige linen for summer, black serge in winter.

Cristobal Balenciaga, who was born in the Basque area of Spain in 1895, ran his own Spanish fashion house, which sold Paris imports as well as his own designs, before relocating to Paris in 1937. In Paris he opened a couture house at 10, avenue Georges V. His most influential designs, year in and year out, were his most subtle and strict, but he was also admired for his passementerie, ball fringes, and Spanish laces; for color combinations like cinnamon, hot pink, iced aquamarine, or creamy white with black; and for shapes that ranged from bubbles and balloons to free-form billowing sails. Balenciaga styles, which reigned over fashion until he closed his house in 1968, included variations on the chemise, sometimes with tunic or overblouse; unfitted suits, especially those whose collars pulled away from the base of the neck in back; and evening clothes that relied on shape and cut rather than embellishment for impact.

Pierre Balmain

In 1945 Pierre Balmain opened his own couture house in Paris and was immediately heralded by American *Vogue* as the newest French sensation. As one of the top couturiers, for decades Balmain consistently came up with elegant, flattering, and pretty clothes. One of his silhouettes was specifically known as "Jolie Madame," but any of them could have also been thus described. Balmain was more involved with costuming for the movies than any of his colleagues; his credits run into the dozens. Perhaps his favorite actress was the deliciously feminine and witty Kay Kendall, whom he dressed for *The Reluctant Debutante*, among other roles.

Balmain was born in 1904 near Aix-les-Bains in France. His father, who died when he was seven, had been involved with a wholesale fabric business and his mother had once worked in a boutique. As a widow she returned to running a boutique, and Balmain grew up playing with scraps of materials and reading in fashion magazines about couturiers like Doucet, Poiret, and Patou. Early influences also included Madame Premet and Madame Becker of Bernard et Cie, both in charge of well-regarded couture houses. Although he knew he wanted to work in the couture, he appeased his mother by attending architecture school. While a student he showed sketches to Molyneux, who hired him as an apprentice even after he was called up for his military service. In 1939 he began working for the house of Lucien Lelong, where he stayed off and on until after the war, when he established himself at 44, rue François I. After his death in 1982 the role of couturier was assumed by his former assistant, Erik Mortensen.

Pierre Cardin

Pierre Cardin had been a couturier in charge of his own house in Paris for seven years when he was suddenly discovered (in 1957) by the American press and hailed for his youthful, avant-garde designs. Although he worked within the confines of the narrow-waisted, full-skirted New Look silhouette, he also experimented throughout the fifties with more relaxed shapes: versions of what would come to be known as the sack dress, with variously raised or lowered waistlines and fitted fronts paired with ballooning backs, often made in bold, heavy tweeds. During the sixties his imagination ran wild. He designed backless evening dresses with silk flowers nestled into low cowls, pop-art appliquéd mini-dresses, knitted dresses molded with three-dimensional patterns reminiscent of egg cartons, clothes suspended from molded metal body jewelry, dresses and tunics held out by hula-hoop-sized wires, dresses with see-through cutouts, and since he was designing for both men and women, unisex ensembles featuring ribbed turtleneck bodysuits with low-slung trousers or tunics.

Cardin was born in 1922 in Venice, but soon returned to France with his family. He began work at the age of fourteen, when he was apprenticed to a tailor. During World War II he served with the Red Cross and afterwards worked for the couture houses of Paquin, Marcelle Chaumont, and Schiaparelli. When Dior was assembling his own house, in 1946, he hired Cardin, and there he remained for three years before leaving to strike out on his own. By 1954 he was already involved with boutiques and with ready-to-wear designing;

these ventures have grown so phenomenally that the vast quantity and range in quality of his licensing arrangements have eclipsed his couture designs, which remain very much entrenched in his 1960s signature looks.

Chanel

Of all the couturiers who ever plied their trade, Gabrielle Chanel can be considered the most successful. She believed in style as opposed to fashion, and style is what she provided for her like-minded customers from before World War I until the start of World War II, when she retired, and from 1954, when she reopened her rue Cambon couture house, until her death in 1971. So appropriate was her own personal style to modern women and so appealingly easy to wear, that it has again come to the forefront of fashion, as led by Karl Lagerfeld, who took over designing for the by-then moribund house in 1984. Copies of Chanel clothes and accessories abound, and not just in the traditionally unimaginative lowest rung of ready-to-wear, but on into the haute couture.

Chanel's innovations can be summed up by mention of a very few garments—the three-piece suit, the little-nothing short evening dress, the tailored long dress—as well as by a handful of accessories, like her two-toned sling-back shoes, chain-handled quilted pocketbooks, silk lapel flowers (preferably camellias), boater hats, jewelry of molten glass and baroque faux pearls set in heavy gilt metal with chains, and, of course, one of her perfumes. Within these limited parameters Chanel, and those inspired by her, produced endless variations on a theme; whether designed in the teens, twenties, thirties, fifties, sixties, or eighties, they were never slavishly reflective of their particular epoch. Chanel's clothes could be and were worn by all types of women from the most chic *belle-laide* to great feminine beauties like Suzy Parker, one of her favorite models. They were also suitable for all ages, beginning at about twenty-one and extending seven or so decades. It is telling about her breadth of vision that Chanel could be so popular with so many generations all at once.

André Courrèges

Mini-skirts, go-go boots, and hip-hugger pants, perhaps the three most definitive sartorial items of the sixties, all made their couture debuts in the 1963 and 1964 collections of André Courrèges. While Courrèges did not invent the mini-skirt, his version, almost always flared from a slightly raised or lowered and unfitted waistline, did become one of the most-worn looks of the decade, along with his equally youthful flat-soled mid-calf boots and his navel-baring stovepipe trousers.

Courrèges, who was born in the Basque region of France in 1923, studied civil engineering, worked for a tailor, and served as a pilot during World War II before finally discovering his vocation during the eleven years he worked for Balenciaga. He opened his own couture house at 48, avenue Kléber in 1961. Almost immediately, his perfectly cut simple suits and coats were influential, accessorized with either his short boots or mary janes, gloves, and hats that managed to combine the styles of astronaut helmet and baby bonnet. Typical Courrèges designs were strictly tailored dresses or coats or pants made in whimsical materials like appliquéd organdy or heavy machine-made lace. He favored heavy materials with lots of body, sometimes very thick, as in the dress and jacket that Madame Claude (Paris's most renowned madam) was wearing when she was shot in the shoulder; her Courrèges ensemble stopped the bullet.

Christian Dior

Christian Dior's first collection under his own name, shown in 1947, was so shockingly luxurious that it was mind-boggling; the world heard all about the New Look seemingly within moments after it was first shown at 30, avenue Montaigne. All credit for reviving the couture after World War II was given to Dior, despite the resumption of couture showings two years earlier and the production of plenty of beautiful and feminine clothes during that time. During World War II the world had begun to think of fashion as being somewhat scattered, as something that could be produced in New York, California, or London as well as in Paris. Dior managed to provide fashion with leadership, and in doing so reconfirmed that the French couture was the apex of fashion.

Christian Dior was born in Granville, France, in 1905. After studying political science, he opened an art gallery in Paris in 1928, which would fail to survive the depression that followed the 1929 crash. After family tragedies, and a severe illness of his own, Dior began a new career in 1935 selling fashion sketches to various milliners and couturiers. In 1938 he went to work for Robert Piguet, but he was drafted into the French army the following year. In 1941 he was hired as an assistant designer by Lucien Lelong, and there he remained until 1946, when Marcel Boussac of the Boussac textile company offered to back him in a couture house of his own. In the decade that followed, Dior produced two collections a year, each with a theme that embodied its slightly different, or very different, silhouette. Women around the world knew to watch Dior for the proper new hemline, or waistline placement. By 1955 Dior's assistant, Yves Saint Laurent, was providing design input; when Dior died in 1957 Saint Laurent would succeed him, but only to design two collections before being drafted. His replacement was Marc Bohan, who, like Dior, had worked for Robert Piguet and was then an assistant at Molyneux for five years before going over to Dior.

Givenchy

Hubert de Givenchy burst onto the scene of the aftermath of the New Look and, with a first collection designed primarily in cotton poplin, breathed fresh air into the somewhat baroque post-war couture scene. Because he was unable to afford more expensive fabrics, Givenchy used the poplin for everything from ruffled evening capes to blouses and skirts. Much of his collection was based on the idea of separates that could be worn in a variety of combinations, and Givenchy's fresh young ideas were an immediate success.

Givenchy was born in 1927 in Beauvais, France. Beginning in 1944 he worked for Jacques Fath, Robert Piguet, Lucien Lelong, and finally, for four years, for Schiaparelli, where he designed for her boutique. In 1952 he showed his first collection in his own house on the avenue Alfred de Vigny. Within the next two years he would strike up two friendships that would shape his future work. First he met his idol Balenciaga and, especially after he moved his couture house across the street from Balenciaga's on the avenue Georges V, rarely designed anything that didn't show his influence. Although Givenchy continued to work in a young vein, using whimsical prints and patterns, his design became more disciplined and sculptural. In 1954 Givenchy met Audrey Hepburn and began to design her clothes for her movies and for real life as well. More than thirty-five years later, their collaboration of couturier and muse still provides the world with one of its most potent images of elegance.

Madame Grès

Unlike most women designers, who tend to produce only the kind of clothes they themselves like to wear, Madame Grès works not just within the confines of her own taste but instead with an allegiance to an artistic aesthetic. For more than fifty years, as Alix Barton, then as Alix, and finally as Grès, she has created clothes that express her own vision of the female form and of the possibilities inherent in the play of fabric upon that form.

Born Germaine Barton, Madame Grès wanted to be a sculptress but ended up training with the small couture house of Premet in the late twenties before starting her own house in 1930 with the new first name of Alix. Her clothes, which were very much in tune with 1930s fashion in that they highlighted the natural figure, were also innovative. Inventions of Alix in the thirties included the strapless evening dress and the diaper-wrapped bathing suit. After a dispute with her backers she lost the rights to the name Alix. When she reopened, at 1, rue de la Paix, her new name was Grès, which she borrowed from her painter-husband.

Grès continued to work with her specially woven matte silk jersey, making intricately draped sculptural dresses, and in stiff paper taffeta or faille for dresses with bubble shapes, harem hems, or origami-folded lines, as well as in most other materials for day dresses, playclothes, sportswear, and, one of her specialties, at-home clothes. During the forties and fifties she was known for never having resorted to shoulder pads or boning; so beautifully draped and constructed were her clothes that they didn't need any extra interior supports to hold their shapes.

Christian Lacroix

At a time when the pertinence of the couture's existence is being questioned, Christian Lacroix serves to remind the fashion world that relevance isn't everything. Lacroix's poufs and other fantasy concoctions have not been any more outlandish and controversial than Poiret's wired tunics over hobble skirts, Schiaparelli's surrealist accessories, Dior's New Look, or the 1960s street- and space-age-inspired creations of Saint Laurent, Courrèges, and Cardin. That the couture is a laboratory of ideas doesn't mean that all of its ideas have to be realistic. Some, like Lacroix's, can be more visual than functional.

Christian Lacroix was born in 1950. With the intention of one day becoming a museum curator, he studied at the Musée du Louvre and the Sorbonne but decided instead to go into fashion design and was hired by Hermès. Next he went to work for the house of Jean Patou, where, as his collections became more and more dramatic, his reputation soared. In 1987 he left Patou, ostensibly because he was frustrated at not being able to work with ready-to-wear, and opened his own house in the Faubourg St.-Honoré, where he designs couture, luxe ready-to-wear, lesser-priced ready-to-wear, and accessories.

Jeanne Lanvin

The house of Lanvin, which in 1990 will have been in existence for one hundred years, was established by Jeanne Lanvin, who began by making millinery and then branched out into designing children's clothes as well as clothes for the children's mothers. Until her death in 1946, when her daughter, the comtesse de Polignac, took over, Jeanne Lanvin specialized in evening clothes, *tailleurs*, lingerie, and accessories that ran the gamut from romantic and youthful *robes de style* to the most sophisticated of evening clothes and sportswear. In 1950 the couture house hired Antonio del Castillo as its couturier, and for the next thirteen years his label would appear alongside that of Lanvin. Castillo, born in Madrid in 1908, had worked for Robert Piguet and for Paquin before moving to New York to run the couture salon at Elizabeth Arden during World War II.

Like Lanvin's, Castillo's designs were unabashedly romantic. They typically were made in dashing, vibrant-colored materials with fichu or off-the-shoulder necklines and such details as large-scale embroideries and scalloped edges. After Castillo left to start his own house, Jules-François Crahay became the Lanvin couturier. Crahay was born in Liège, Belgium, in 1917, and studied fashion design in Paris before returning to his home town to run his mother's couture house. He was a prisoner of war from 1940 to 1945, after which he returned to Paris, where he briefly ran his own couture house and then went to work at Nina Ricci. By 1950 he was designing under his own name for Ricci. Crahay was an innovative couturier, basing collections on themes having to do with Russia, India, or Peru for clothes that featured bloomer, dhoti, or gaucho pants, oversized prints and ornaments of feathers, loops of self-piping, or organdy ruffs. Upon his retirement in 1984 Maryll Lanvin, wife of the son of the cousin of Jeanne Lanvin's daughter, who for several years had been designing Lanvin *prêt-à-porter*, became the house couturiere as well.

Maggy Rouff

The house of Maggy Rouff was known for delightful, feminine clothes usually made with an amusing or eye-catching twist in silhouette, color, or ornamentation. It was begun in 1929 when Maggy Besançon de Wagner took over her parents' couture house, Drecoll, which was relocating as it merged with the house of Beer. She changed her name to Rouff, and opened for business at 136, avenue des Champs Elysées. She continued designing until she retired in 1948, when her daughter became the couturiere and the business moved to the avenue Matignon. In the sixties the business moved again, first to the avenue Marceau, then to the avenue Montaigne. Its designers included Jean Marie Armand, Serge Matta, and Guy Douvier.

Yves Saint Laurent

In the more than thirty years he has been a couturier, Yves Saint Laurent has consistently managed to merge fantasy with practicality. Even in his Russian-peasant-, African-, and Picasso-inspired collections, unusual embroideries and patchworks, and fabulous color and material combinations have been interpreted in the most classical and wearable of silhouettes. His impeccable pantsuits, day dresses, and "smokings" have for decades determined how women look when not in ballgowns.

Yves Saint Laurent was born in Algeria in 1936. At the age of seventeen he won first prize for a dress design in a contest sponsored by the International Wool Secretariat and, after briefly attending fashion design school, went to work for Christian Dior. By 1955 his designs were being included in Dior's couture collections. When Dior died in 1957, Saint

Laurent was hired as his successor. After two collections he was drafted to serve in the army and the house replaced him with another Dior assistant, Marc Bohan. In 1962, Yves Saint Laurent opened his own house in the rue Spontini, relocating in 1974 to the avenue Marceau.

Emanuel Ungaro

Emanuel Ungaro was born in 1933 in Aix-les-Provence. While still quite young he went to work for his father, who, with his four other sons, ran a local tailoring shop. Thus Ungaro was already trained when, in 1958, he took a job as tailoring assistant to Balenciaga, where he stayed six years. In 1964 he quit to work with Courrèges, another Balenciaga alumnus, but after a year he decided to open his own couture house, which he did in 1965 with the print designer Sonia Knapp.

Ungaro's first designs, which were immediately popular, were not unlike those of Courrèges. Ungaro designed peppy suits and coats with bright contrasting bands for trim, transparent jumpsuits of organdy with three-dimensional appliqués, dresses with matching boots, and low-slung trousers paired with back-baring tops. Most of his designs were avant-garde, such as a beaten brass mini-skirt paired with a bare breastplate hung with chains and a peace symbol. By 1971 Ungaro, who had relocated in 1967 to the avenue Montaigne and had the following year branched out into ready-to-wear, began to find his own specific signature. This was based both on the idea of layering different elements together in a single costume that could then be worn in many ways, and on combining the various prints that Sonia Knapp had designed to complement each other. These prints ranged from complex geometrics worked out in a variety of subtle colorways to large-scale, hand-painted-looking abstracts. The ensembles played proportions against each other as well as various patterns and textures. By the eighties Ungaro was continuing to work with mixing elements, and the elements themselves were becoming more luxurious; by the middle of the decade he was playing soft fluid shirring against the more tailored lines of jackets and coats.

Caroline Rennolds Milbank is an independent costume scholar.

GLOSSARY OF TEXTILE TERMS

BENGALINE: A lustrous, ribbed cloth of warp-faced plain weave. The ribs are created by coupling a fine warp with a thick, soft weft.

BROCADE: A textile patterned with a supplementary weft secured in the ground weave. These supplementary wefts are discontinuous, appearing only where required by the pattern, and not carried from selvage to selvage. Brocade is also a term often used to denote a rich, figured silk, whether or not it is patterned using the above method.

CHANTILLY LACE: Originally an eighteenth-century, black bobbin lace produced in Chantilly, in northeastern France. The name is now generally applied to floral-patterned black laces, both hand- and machine-made.

CHIFFON: A lightweight, diaphanous, plain-weave fabric made of fine, hard-twisted threads.

CHINA SILK: A plain-weave, lustrous, lightweight silk fabric produced in China and Japan. Often used for blouses, lingerie, and linings.

CHINÉ: Patterned fabric with warp and/or weft threads that have been printed or resist-dyed before weaving begins, giving the pattern soft or fuzzy outlines. Also known as clouded and, when referring to resist-dyed threads, as ikat.

CLOQUÉ: A fabric with an irregularly raised, "blistered" surface; often a doublecloth.

CREPE: A fabric woven of extremely hard-twisted threads, either single or plied, and characterized by a crinkled or grained surface effect.

DOUBLECLOTH: A two-layer fabric, each layer with its own set of warps and wefts. The layers interconnect at intervals by the exchange of certain warps or wefts between them, or alternatively can be connected by a separate set of binding elements. The technique is often used to create a reversible fabric with an identical pattern in opposite colors on each face.

DOUBLEKNIT: A firm fabric of loops interlocked with a double stitch using two needles.

FAILLE: A plain-weave, flat-ribbed fabric, slightly stiff and lustrous. The ribs are created by using a slightly heavier thread in the weft than in the warp.

GABARDINE: A tightly woven, warp-faced twill fabric with closely set surface ribs.

GAZAR: A stiff, stretchy, openwork silk doublecloth, one face in plain weave, the other in gauze weave.

GEORGETTE: A sheer, plain-weave crepe fabric with a fine-textured, matte surface.

GRAIN DE POUDRE: The finest gauge of gabardine.

GROSGRAIN: A firm, ribbed fabric of warp-faced plain weave with either a matte or slightly shiny surface. The ribs, rounder than those in faille, derive from a fine warp coupled with a heavier weft. Often used as ribbon.

GUIPURE: The term, in use as early as the late seventeenth century, has been associated with a variety of different laces. In its broadest sense it denotes laces with large patterns, usually made with bars (struts of thread used to link motifs together) instead of a mesh ground.

JERSEY: A general term denoting a plain, knitted fabric without a distinct rib. Jersey was originally made only of wool, but now appears in a variety of other materials, including silk.

ORGANZA: A sheer, plain-weave fabric with a stiff finish.

OTTOMAN: A firm, lustrous, warp-faced plain-weave fabric with large, round ribs (larger than bengaline).

PAILLETTES: The French term for sequins or spangles, it is sometimes used in English to denote non-disk-shaped sequins.

PAPER TAFFETA: A lightweight taffeta with a particularly crisp, paperlike handle.

RAFFIA: A leaf stalk fiber obtained from the raffia palm, native to Madagascar.

RATTINE: A thick, napped wool or wool and cotton twill fabric. The cloth is rubbed during the finishing process, giving it a nubby surface.

RAW SILK: Fabric produced from unprocessed (filaments still completely or partially coated with gum sericin, deposited by the silkworm), untwisted silk thread.

SATIN: A term referring both generally to a fabric characterized by a smooth, lustrous, silky surface, and specifically to a simple float weave, usually warp-faced. Each warp floats over a minimum of four wefts and under only one weft, and the starting points of the floats are staggered to create a smooth, unbroken surface.

SHANTUNG: A rough-textured, plain-weave fabric that is usually produced with uneven wefts. The unevenness is the result of knots, lumps, and other imperfections left in the thread.

SOUTACHE: A narrow twill braid, used as trimming.

TAFFETA: A crisp, usually lustrous, plain-weave silk fabric with a fine weft-wise rib.

TULLE: A fine, machine-made net with a hexagonal mesh.

TWEED: A class of wool fabrics characterized by a rough, often hairy, surface and a soft texture. Tweeds come in a variety of weaves, but are most often twill variations.

TWILL: A type of float weave in which the float extends over a group of two or more and then under one or more units of the opposite set. The warp grouping shifts one warp beyond the previous group for each successive weft, creating a strong, characteristic diagonal.

UTILITY WEAR: Clothing produced in Britain from 1942–1954 under the wartime sumptuary laws that rationed the amount of fabric and trim that could be used for each garment. Top British designers, such as Norman Hartnell and Hardy Amies, designed the line, but by the end of rationing, Utility wear had become a reminder of the unpleasantness of wartime.

VELVET: A pile fabric. The pile is created by an extra warp raised into loops and anchored in the ground weave. The loops may be cut, uncut, or a combination of the two.

VOILE: A sheer, open plain-weave fabric woven with hard-twist threads. Voile has a crisp, wiry handle.

ZIBELINE: A lustrous silk twill fabric usually made with thick, untwisted wefts and fine twisted warps. A variation using untwisted warps and wefts of equal weight is also known.

Photo Credits

Additional works of art from the collections of The Fine Arts Museums of San Francisco appear in the photographs of the following costumes:

No. 2. Robert Henri, American, *O in Black With Scarf (Marjorie Henri)*, 1910, oil on canvas, Gift of The de Young Museum Society, purchased with funds donated by the Charles E. Merrill Trust.

No. 6. Giovanni Boldini, Italian, *Portrait of Mrs. Whitney Warren, Sr.*, oil on canvas, Bequest of Whitney Warren, Jr., in memory of Mrs. Adolph Spreckels.

No. 9. Gustave Doré, French, *Vase: Poème de la Vigne*, 1877–78, bronze, Gift of M. H. de Young.

Nos. 10, 11; no. 14. *Painted Paneled Room*, Italian, Tirano, late 18th century, wood, M. H. de Young Endowment Fund.

No. 13. *The Poultry Market*, Flemish, Brussels, 1765–94, attr. Jan van Orley and Augustin Coppens, wool and silk, Gift of the M. H. de Young Endowment Fund.

No. 22. *Louis XV Room*, France, Rouen, 1735–40, gilt oak, Roscoe and Margaret Oakes Collection.

No. 25. Jean-Marc Nattier, French, *Thalia, Muse of Comedy (Silvia Balletti?)*, 1739, oil on canvas, Mildred Anna Williams Collection.

No. 30. *Cabinet on Stand*, French, Paris, after 1641, ebony, attr. to Jean Macé, Gift of William Randolph Hearst.

No. 32. (left to right) *Suit of Armor*, Germany, Nuremberg, ca. 1515, steel, and *Suit of Armor*, made by Anton Peffenhauser, Germany, Augsburg, ca. 1540, steel, both Gift of the William Randolph Hearst Foundation; *Suit of Armor*, Germany, Augsburg, ca. 1540, steel, Gift of Mrs. Archer M. Huntington; *Suit of Armor*, Germany, Nuremberg, ca. 1515, steel, Gift of the William Randolph Hearst Foundation.

No. 34. Workshop of Benvenuto Cellini, Italian, Florence, *Portrait Bust of Cosimo I de' Medici*, ca. 1548–53, marble, Roscoe and Margaret Oakes Collection.

Nos. 37, 39. *Johann von Wespien Room*, Johann Joseph Couven, (1701–68), Germany, Aachen, ca. 1740, oak, Museum Purchase, Gift of various donors.

No. 40; no. 105. Persia/Iran, Fars Province, Qashqa'i, *Carpet*, wool, Bequest of H. McCoy Jones.

No. 51; no. 78. *Rabbit-hunting with Ferrets*, Franco-Flemish, 1460–70, wool and silk, M. H. de Young Endowment Fund.

No. 53. *Choir Stalls*, European, 17th century, walnut, Gift of the de Young Museum Society.

No. 59; no. 70. Wallpaper panels, *Savages of the Pacific Ocean*, designed by Jean-Gabriel Charvet, painted by Joseph Dufour, French, Mâcon, ca. 1806, block print on paper, Gift of Georgia M. Worthington and The Fine Arts Museums Trustees Fund.

No. 81. *Wall Fountain*, European, 16th century, marble, Museum purchase, Salinger Bequest Fund.

No. 83. *Large-leaved Verdure*, Flemish, possibly Grammont, 1550–60, wool, Gift of Charles de Limur and his sister, Mary Ethel Weinmann.

Nos. 84, 85, 92, 96; nos. 87, 88. *The Creation and The Fall of Man*, from *The Redemption of Man* tapestry series, Flemish, Brussels, 1510–15, wool and silk, Gift of the William Randolph Hearst Foundation.

Nos. 89, 90. *The Audience of the Emperor*, from *The Story of the Emperor of China* tapestry series, French, Beauvais, before 1732, designed by Guy Louis de Vernansal, Belin de Fontenay, and probably Jean-Baptiste Monnoyer, wool and silk, Gift of the Roscoe and Margaret Oakes Foundation.

No. 95. William Wetmore Story, American, *Dalilah*, 1877, marble, Gift of M. H. de Young.

Photographs: Kaz Tsuruta